Iowa Gardener's Travel Guide

*Janet Mayer
2009*

Kelly D. Norris

First published in 2008 by
Culicidae Architectural Press
an imprint of Culicidae Press, LLC
918 5th Street
Ames, IA 50010-5906
USA

www.cularchpress.com

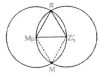

Culicidae Architectural Press

Ames | Berlin | Gainesville | Tokyo

IOWA GARDENER'S TRAVEL GUIDE. Copyright © 2008 by Kelly D. Norris. All rights reserved. No part of this book may be reproduced in any form by any electronic or mechanized means (including photocopying, recording, or information storage and retrieval) without written permission, except in the case of brief citations embodied in critical articles and reviews. For information address Culicidae Architectural Press, 918 5th Street, Ames, IA 50010, USA or email to cularchpress@gmail.com

ISBN-13: 978-1-4357-5039-5

Cover photos by Kelly D. Norris © 2008
Cover design by mikeschDesign.com © 2008
Book layout and design by 9one8Design.com © 2008
All interior images are © by Kelly D. Norris
Author image © Meredith Corporation, Des Moines, IA

Table of Contents

Dedication	4
Acknowledgments	5
Introduction	6
How-To Use Guide	8
Northwest Iowa	9
Other Places of Interest in the NW Iowa Region	37
Your Day Trip Planner for Northwest Iowa	40
Northeast Iowa	43
Other Places of Interest in the NE Iowa Region	83
Your Day Trip Planner for Northeast Iowa	87
Southwest Iowa	93
Other Places of Interest in the SW Iowa Region	103
Your Day Trip Planner for Southwest Iowa	104
Southeast Iowa	107
Other Places of Interest in the SE Iowa Region	126
Your Day Trip Planner for Southeast Iowa	129
Central Iowa	133
Other Places of Interest in the Central Iowa Region	164
Your Day Trip Planner for Central Iowa	168

Dedication

i thank You God for most this amazing day

And it's with a greenly spirit and a blue true dream that I dedicate this to those whom I've shared company with in this great life.

Acknowledgments

A project of this sort often involves more the efforts of others than the author would candidly like to admit. Nonetheless, credit is due where credit is due. I would be sitting at a desk pondering my next step had it not been for James Baggett's cheering words on that riverboat cruise in Montreal in the summer of 2006. "Go for it. I think it's your best idea yet", meant as much then as it does now. Here's to going for it.

This book isn't perfect and no amount of finessing would satisfy my perfectionist leanings. The topic is anomalous, multi-faceted, and has been carried on in a variety of forms by other authors in other parts of the country. These authors have elected more conventional approaches whereby exercising the full measure of their wit by including lists, lists, and more lists, cheery little essays, helpful tips sections, and a whole lot of information that clouds the scope, at least to me. This is a travel guide, Iowa's travel guide to Iowa's gardens and nurseries. And it's been written by a writer with journalistic inklings. Opinionated I may be, but that should bear little on the adventure you and your traveling companions wish to embark on in search of great plants, great nurseries, and great gardens. I've refrained from personal remarks that might cloud any firm's reputation or cause the reader to second guess a decision to visit. That's not my call. Besides in this industry, the good and honest survive while the shady and poorly managed subside. My editor and life sibling Lindsey Smith has held the reins on such journalistic purview. Her careful copy editing skills marked with a razor-edged opinion have rounded off this work into something I can feel good about. I couldn't have done it without her.

Of course this whole business of writing a travel guide wouldn't have been necessary if not for an early appreciation for travel instilled by my grandparents (both maternal and paternal). But my maternal grandmother, Cheryl Johnson, was the one who summer after summer toted my brother and me around the Midwest in search of something cultural about the place where we lived. She catered these excursions to her grandsons' unique interests - gardens and nurseries for me and toy-tractor shops and racecar museums for my brother. If we could find it, we'd visit. And we found a lot!

I'd start this paragraph with finally but I'm sure I've forgotten many much deserving people. It's easy to do but not intended with slight. Deb Wiley, friends late at night over glasses (or bottles) of wine, the business owners who've put up with inquiry letters, forms, reminder cards, and emails, my advisor Cindy Haynes who's put up with more than this travel guide, the ISU Honors Program for funding support, Susan Appleget-Hurst for her efforts before mine and her always wise and considerate counsel, Mikesch Muecke for his patience, guidance, and creative genius, and a million others who shall thus remain nameless.

Introduction

The land between two rivers, that which Iowans call home, is a cache of beautiful gardens. Tormented with a fitful climate prone to teasing, fleeting hints of spring in March, surprise snow in April, sporadic mid-May freezes, torrential rains and storms in July, and bitterly cold wind chills in January, these gardens are as resilient as they are ravishing. Created by people as different as coal and diamonds, the gardens and nurseries of Iowa featured in this book share a common thread: they exist out of undying passion for plants, people, and the outdoor world. These horticultural retreats offer the visitor a plethora of opportunities to experience an immense diversity of plants and endless ways of using them. Some sell plants. Others simply take pleasure in their cultivation. Whatever the niche, these gardens are true expressions of their creators. To know a garden is to know its creator.

The purpose of this book is to offer the reader the chance to explore, experience, and discover the public and private gardens and nurseries in Iowa. I have had the good fortune to visit many of these over the last ten years and must say that the horticultural entities of this state will prove amazing for those who have yet to embark on a quest to see them. The spirit of travel has followed me my whole life. But traveling to see gardens was something fostered by my maternal grandmother on little escapades around the state to see what else, gardens and nurseries. Whether at the private homes of hospitable women glad to open their garden gate to a budding green thumb or tucked-away little nurseries on backcountry roads, our travels took us to some of the finest gardens and nurseries that I've had the pleasure of visiting. It is my goal to share them with you in a succinctly written guide that leads you on adventures much like I've had.

The book is divided into five geographic regions. Each of the four quadrants (Northwest, Northeast, Southwest, Southeast), delineated by the Interstate 35 and Interstate 80 transection of the state, are included as well as a fifth region from the heart of the state (Central). This convenient division will allow the reader to easily and efficiently find places worth visiting in any given area of the state. The geographic organization will also give the gardener-traveler a chance to experience what gardening is like across Iowa. In addition to this, the book also seeks to provide budding gardeners an insight into the gems of their immediate locality. Many who have only been bitten by the gardening bug may have yet to peruse the great gardens and nurseries of their area. Toting this guide along is surely a wise first step.

Travelers of the green persuasion from outside Iowa will also find the information contained herein valuable if a summer vacation must include a stop of horticultural interest (and what vacation couldn't?). Visitors to the state will get to experience first hand the fruits of many dedicated gardeners' labors and the interest the people of this state have in maintaining an aesthetically pleasing quality of life. The destinations profiled in this book cover the gamut of gardening. Each full-length entry offers a brief glimpse of what you can expect. I've asked these retail establishments to tell me a little something about who they are, what their specialties are, and even what their favorite plant is. After all to know a creator of gardens is to know the gardens they create. Other entries for which we were unable to garner complete details are listed in a truncated directory at the end of each section for easy locating. These are well worth a visit too.

This book isn't perfect and thanks to a technological age, your input will allow me and my team to keep this as up-to-date as possible. This book is not a periodical but will be republished every few years as is absolutely necessary to keep the data relevant. Have we not covered a local plant shop near your home? Maybe we've missed that favorite out-of-the-way nursery that has great-looking stuff each spring. Let us know by visiting www.iowagardenersbook.com! Your input will allow this guide to stay as comprehensive as possible.

In closing I suppose I can't put it any more plainly when I say that this book is for you. It's the Iowa gardener's desk reference for places to go, see, and enjoy. So catch the travel bug. Buy a plant or two. Seek inspiration in gardens afield. At any rate, hit the road and go gardening!

How-To Use Guide

Contact information: The necessary information for getting ahold of a location of interest. Emails and addresses have been provided when available.

Sense of place: Iowa is a beautiful place to live and garden. It's nice to be reminded of the beauty of our state especially when travelling.

Do they charge admission? This way you can know how much money is left to spend on plants and other gardener must-haves.

When are they there? Many of Iowa's businesses are open seasonally. Always call ahead before visiting to confirm dates and times. The first line indicates the days of the week they're open. The second line lists the hours for each day in the same order as the first line, delineated by commas.

Get to know them: It's always nice to know a little something about the people and places you visit. Here you'll find historical information and any relevant trivia.

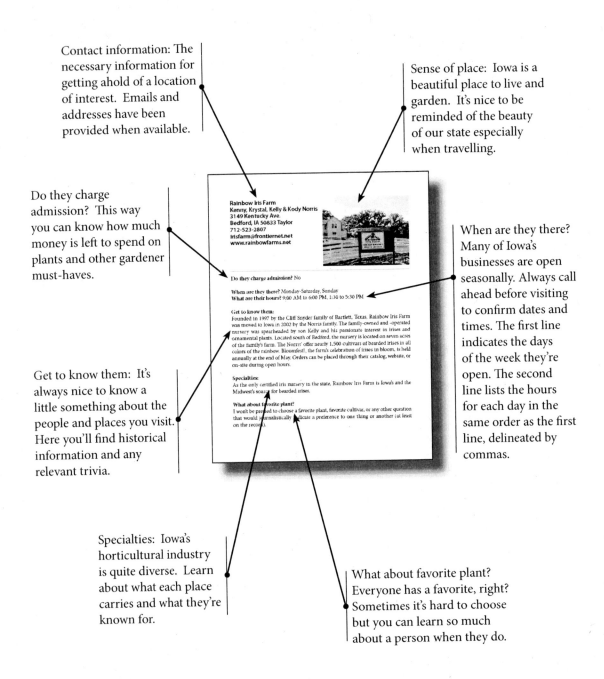

Specialties: Iowa's horticultural industry is quite diverse. Learn about what each place carries and what they're known for.

What about favorite plant? Everyone has a favorite, right? Sometimes it's hard to choose but you can learn so much about a person when they do.

8

Northwest Iowa

Some say you can't wander too far astray in Northwest Iowa without finding someone with a Dutch last name. Outposts of Old World culture like Orange City endow this northerly district of our state with a strong sense of heritage. For gardeners it gives way to our treasurable floral heritage, what I think is one of the most tenuous elements of modern society.

But here you'll find that cause alive and well. Gardens with barns, sheds, and otherwise forgotten buildings of yesteryear are found between tall rows of corn and soybeans that seem to stretch endlessly save the occasional wind turbine. Several of my favorites carry a do-good assortment of old-fashioned ornamentals that add charm to any yard.

Traveling around Northwest Iowa is simple and filled with getaway places, even after all the gardens and nurseries have been taken in. Spend an evening watching the sunset in the bluffs or a day in the water at Lake Okoboji. Either way you'll catch the spirit that keeps bringing me back.

Northwest Iowa

NW

Becker's Garden Center
Jeff Becker
1335 1st Avenue North
Fort Dodge, IA 50501 *Webster*
515-576-6671

When are they there? Year-round. Monday-Friday, Saturday, Sunday
What are their hours? 8:00 AM to 7:00 PM, 8:00 AM to 5:00 PM, noon to 4:00 PM

Get to know them:
Becker Florist and Garden Center is a full-service flower and plant shop offering a large selection of perennials and potted trees and shrubs. Assorted annuals in packs and hanging baskets are offered in the spring. They also carry an extensive selection of foliage plants in their flower shop.

Specialties:
Bedding plants, perennials, trees, and shrubs for sale in addition to a flower shop.

Central Gardens of North Iowa
800 2nd Avenue North, P.O. Box 735
Clear Lake, IA 50428 *Cerro Gordo*
641-357-0700
centralgardens@netins.net
www.central-gardens.org

When are they there? Seasonally. April through October. Call for specific open days.
What are their hours? Dawn to dusk

Get to know them:
Central Gardens of North Iowa is a 2.75-acre facility with 22 theme gardens located in the heart of Clear Lake. This multi-community venture has resulted in hundreds of volunteers contributing their time to the garden each summer. The garden attracts over 16,000 visitors each summer who come to see displays like the bird garden, wetland garden, pond garden, wildflower garden, and ornamental grass garden.

Specialties:
Northern Iowa's only public garden is host to many activities throughout the summer including a garden tour, plant sales, and an evening of music and entertainment called GardenFest's Garden Gala. This is a public garden for the whole family.

NW

Cottage Gardens
Roger DeVries
805 21st Street
Milford, IA 51351 *Dickinson*
712-338-4569
info@cottagegardens.net
www.cottagegardens.net

When are they there? Seasonally. April-October. Monday-Sunday.
What are their hours? 9:00 AM to 5:00 PM. Extended hours in May.

Get to know them:
Cottage Gardens is a retailer of fine plants and serves the Iowa Great Lakes region, residents and visitors alike. Established in 1998 with only a hobby greenhouse, Cottage Gardens has grown physically and in the local gardening community as well. Armed with experience and a loyal following of satisfied customers, the staff at Cottage Gardens puts together a wide array of beautiful, fast-selling hanging baskets and containers.

Specialties:
This northwest Iowa garden stop is a source of quality annuals, perennials, and shrubs. Vegetable and ornamental containers as well as hanging baskets are particularly worth checking out if you're stopping by.

What about favorite plant?
Owner Roger DeVries says he's enamored with Wave® Petunias. "Their all-season color with low maintenance is hard to beat". And who could disagree? Wave® Petunias have turned the bedding plant world on its head.

Country Gardens Nursery & Landscape
Tony & Jody Cink
2003 230th Street
Wesley, IA 50483 *Hancock*
515-679-4234
tjcink@awcmail.com

When are they there? Seasonally. Open last week of April. Tuesday-Saturday.
What are their hours? 9:00 AM to 5:00 PM

Get to know them:
Located at their acreage, Tony and Jody Cink have been in business for 10 years supplying north central Iowa gardeners and do-it-yourselfers with the tools, plants, and supplies for any home landscaping job. Established flower beds around their home give customers a chance to see plants at work. Plus the kids have their own area, too, complete with chickens, goats, ducks, and sometimes geese. According to Jody "there is lots for all to enjoy on your day to the country!"

Specialties:
The Cinks offer a full line of landscape installation services ranging from paver patios to retaining walls. If you're in the mood to do it yourself, they carry bulk rock, mulch, edging, and other landscaping supplies too. A nice selection of annuals and perennials makes this a handy one-stop shop if you're near Wesley.

What about favorite plant?
When asked about her favorite plant, Jody says Joe Pye weed takes the pick. "I love eupatorium (*Eupatorium purpureum*) for its mass of blooms in late summer for all the butterflies!" You'll find it abounding happily around Tony and Jody's home.

Northwest Iowa

NW

Courtyard Gardens
Steve Gruhn
3006 Highway 71
Spirit Lake, IA 51360 *Dickinson*
712-336-4558
sgruhn@ecourtyard.com
www.ecourtyard.com

When are they there? Year-round. Monday-Saturday, Sunday. Closed Sundays in January, February, and March.
What are their hours? 9:00 AM to 6:00 PM, 12:00 to 5:00 PM

Get to know them:
Country Gardens is reportedly the only garden center in Iowa with an attached restaurant, Rio Pizzeria, where the specialty is New York-style pizza. Country Gardens has been in business since 1975 serving the Spirit Lake area with "creative gift ideas to suit any style or budget," says owner Steve Gruhn. Their website features online ordering too, a bonus if you live in the area.

Specialties:
Courtyard Gardens has it all, from fresh floral to nursery trees, shrubs, and a great spring selection of annuals featuring their specialty geraniums.

Crees Garden Center
Dan Crees
2213 College Place
Harlan, IA 51537 *Shelby*
712-755-7612
creesgard@iowatelecom.net

When are they there? Seasonally. March 15-Father's Day. Monday-Friday, Saturday, Sunday.
What are their hours? 8:00 AM to 8:00 PM, 8:00 AM to 7:00 PM, noon to 5:00 PM

Get to know them:
"We've been in business 40 years this year," says owner Dan Crees. "My folks started with a greenhouse they bought from the people who owned the land where Mall of the Bluffs is now in Council Bluffs." Dan and his wife took over after his parents retired and look forward to passing the reins on to one of their children someday. Crees Garden Center is known for helping customers with their gardening questions. Dan adds "if we don't know, we'll find out."

Specialties:
Crees Garden Center offers a full selection of home-grown plants. All aspects of lawn care and landscaping are covered. Knowledgeable staff is a plus too.

What about favorite plant?
Dan says that his favorite plant is easily coleus. "I've liked the leaves since I was a kid."

Northwest Iowa

NW

D & D Greenhouse & More
Dale & Deb Richardson
613 1st Avenue NE
Buffalo Center, IA 50424 *Winnebago*
641-562-2999
dndkids@wctatel.net

When are they there? Seasonally. Monday-Friday, Saturday.
What are their hours? 10:00 AM to 5:00 PM, 9:00 AM to 1:00 PM

Specialties:
Dale and Deb carry an array of seasonal plants, shrubs, vegetables, hanging baskets, and home and garden decor.

What about favorite plant?
Dale and Deb are fond of pansies.

Eddie's Greenhouse
Ed Cassady
7 South 23rd Street
Fort Dodge, IA 50501 *Webster*
515-955-2431

When are they there? Year-round. April-May, December. Monday-Friday, Saturday, Sunday.
What are their hours? 8:00 AM to 8:00 PM, 8:00 AM to 6:00 PM, 10:00 AM to 4:00 PM

Get to know them:
Eddie's Greenhouse began as a basement hobby over 26 years ago and has grown into a 1.5-acre facility. Eddie's carries a range of plant products for your garden and stocks Christmas decorations and supplies in season.

Specialties:
Geraniums, perennials, moss baskets, plant towers, and mixed baskets are but a few of Eddie's specialties.

What about favorite plant?
Poinsettias are favorites at Eddie's. I asked why. "Because we get to see the finished product," says Eddie with pride in his product.

NW

Enchanted Gardens
Gina Bauck
18923 Highway 71 North
Carroll, IA 51401 *Carroll*
712-792-1985
enchantedgardens@mchsi.com

When are they there? Seasonally. April-June. Monday-Friday, Saturday, Sunday. **What are their hours?** 9:00 AM to 8:00 PM, 9:00 AM to 5:00 PM, noon to 5:00 PM

Get to know them:
Enchanted Gardens is a garden center where visitors can just get lost. Eclectic and fun containers and plants abound. Gina and her husband maintain a vibrant selection of hanging baskets, containers, and even offer a planting service for folks who'd like advice on what to do with their outdoor space. Her shop has drawn a steady stream of clients from Omaha and Des Moines and out-of-town customers account for 80 percent of her business. Hop in the car and visit this whimsical business.

Specialties:
"I specialize in breathtaking containers," says Gina. Dedicated to her customer's satisfaction Gina's shop only consists of annuals, perennials, and items to help customers realize "the full potential of decorating their yard or patio," as Gina puts it.

What about favorite plant?
Gina is in love with hibiscus. "It loves the sun and I can bring the tropics to me," says the fan of island and tropical-theme decor.

Northwest Iowa

Green Gables Landscaping
Ann Grimm
407 160th Street
West Bend, IA 50597 *Kossuth*
515-887-5678
jag@ncn.net
www.greengableslandscaping.com

NW

When are they there? Seasonally. Monday-Friday, Saturday.
What are their hours? 9:00 AM to 7:00 PM, 9:00 AM to 5:00 PM.

Get to know them:
Green Gables' motto is "escape the ordinary," a sentiment that discerning gardeners will appreciate. While they are mainly a landscape nursery, they are open to the public in the spring for plant sales. Green Gables offers a full line of landscaping services including deck design and installation, retaining wall construction, and paver patios and sidewalks.

Specialties:
The nursery carries over 300 varieties of perennials each spring in addition to woody ornamentals, bedding plants, and water plants. But landscaping is their specialty. On-site display gardens showcase landscaping possibilities and present design ideas that you can incorporate into your own yard.

19

NW

Greenworld Inc.
Larry Ribbens
309 7th Street NW
Sioux Center, IA 51250 *Sioux*
712-722-2621
gworld@mtcnet.net

When are they there? Year-round. Monday-Saturday.
What are their hours? Call for open hours.

Get to know them:
Greenworld is the place to go in Sioux Center if you're looking for a tree. Owner Larry Ribbens' love of trees is evident from the large selection of plants that he carries.

Specialties:
Landscape design and installation and irrigation installation are specialties. Greenworld also does lawn seeding and sodding.

Ground Effects Landscaping, Garden Center, & Flowers
Justin Schuiteman
2075 South Main Avenue
Sioux Center, IA 51250 *Sioux*
712-722-4600
justin@scgroundeffects.com
www.scgroundeffects.com

NW

When are they there? Year-round. Monday-Saturday.
What are their hours? Call for open hours.

Get to know them:
The business started 10 years ago selling tomatoes from a small greenhouse. That greenhouse was slowly converted to annual and perennial production and now they've even got a flower shop. "Our displays around the garden center are something that we also really put time into to give people more ideas," says owner Justin Schuiteman.

Specialties:
Ground Effects is known for unique plants and the creative ways they display them around their nursery. Justin puts it best when he says "we are always trying to do something out of the ordinary."

What about favorite plant?
Picea abies 'Cupressina'. "It is an awesome evergreen. It only gets 3 feet wide but grows 15-20 feet tall. It's just a great plant."

Northwest Iowa

NW

Marjo's Flowers
Brian & Amy Dreith
3110 255th St., P.O. Box 88
Sac City, IA 50583 *Sac*
712-662-7589
farmerbrd@netscape.net

When are they there? Year-round. Monday-Saturday, Sunday.
What are their hours? 8:00 AM to 5:00 PM, 1:00 PM to 4:00 PM

Get to know them:
Marjo's has been supplying wholesale and retail customers in northwest Iowa with bedding plants since 1967 when it was founded by Marv and Joan Wilkerson who'd bought Leonard's Greenhouse. The Dreiths took it over in 2000 and have upheld a long-standing reputation for high-quality floral products. The Dreiths currently have 19 greenhouses and one acre under production.

Specialties:
Bedding plants are Marjo's specialty in addition to their full-service floral shop.

Northwest Iowa

NW

Natural Plus Nursery
Dave & Linda Hopper
10075 263rd Street
Clear Lake, IA 50428 *Cerro Gordo*
641-357-7495
dave@naturalplusnursery.com
www.naturalplusnursery.com

When are they there? Seasonally. Monday-Sunday.
What are their hours? Call for hours.

Get to know them:
Natural Plus Nursery has been in business for over 30 years. Located on a farmstead near Clear Lake, the nursery building was made mostly from barn boards.

Specialties:
Natural Plus Nursery is a large retail operation that offers both residential and commercial landscaping services. You'll find trees, shrubs, perennials, pond plants, and garden art on a relaxing summer visit to Natural Plus.

What about favorite plant?
Dave and Linda have trouble deciding but say that the new varieties of shrub roses and hydrangeas pique their interest because they are easy to grow and very hardy.

NW

**Panorama Gardens
David & Ilene Olson**
3055 Hwy. 44
Panora, IA 50216 *Guthrie*
800-816-2225
idolfam@netins.net

When are they there? Year-round. Monday-Saturday.
What are their hours? 8:00 AM to 5:00 PM.

Get to know them:
Panorama Gardens has been in business since 1956 serving Guthrie County's floricultural needs with their greenhouse and florist shop.

Northwest Iowa

NW

Picket Fence Greenhouse
Diane Mumm
1129 Ginkgo Road
Portsmouth, IA 51565 *Shelby*
712-744-3266
mumm@fmctc.com
www.countryglowemporiumstore.com/picketfencegreenhouse.html

When are they there? Seasonally. Mid-April to end of June. Monday-Friday, Saturday, Sunday.
What are their hours?
9:00 AM to 7:00 PM, 9:00 AM to 5:00 PM, 1:00 PM to 4:00 PM

Get to know them:
Picket Fence Greenhouse has been in business for over seven years. A shade perennial walk-through garden is in full color from June through September. It's open to the public for browsing and seeing plants in combination with each other.

Specialties:
Picket Fence Greenhouse specializes in unique and unusual plants including perennials, shrubs, hostas, pond plants, and annuals. A container planting service is also available.

What about favorite plant?
Diane says that her favorite perennial is 'Moonbeam' coreopsis while her favorite annuals are vincas (*Catharanthus*). "Both plants bloom all summer up to frost. They love the heat and can tolerate some drought conditions too."

NW

Prairie Path
Phyllis & Alvin Hammer
5168 "S" Avenue
Cherokee, IA 51012 *Pocahontas*
712-225-4940
hammerap@ilechsi.com

Do they charge admission? No

When are they there? Seasonally and by-appointment. Daily.
What are their hours?
Call for open hours.

Specialties:
At the Prairie Path you'll find a native wild prairie with prairie flowers on display. A bed and breakfast is also on-site so that you can stay a while and enjoy the serenity of the countryside.

Northwest Iowa

NW

Prairie Pedlar
Jack & Jane Hogue
1609 270th Street
Odebolt, IA 51458 *Ida*
712-668-4840
jhogue@netins.net
www.prairiepedlar.com

Do they charge admission? No

When are they there? Seasonally. April through October. Monday-Saturday, Sunday.
What are their hours? 11:00 AM to 4:00 PM, 1:00 PM to 4:00 PM.

Get to know them:
Prairie Pedlar is a family venture that has become a passion and lifestyle for Jack and Jane Hogue and their three children Janna, Tyler, and Emily. Established in 1985, they've been featured in four national magazines. This oasis in the country is a popular place for weddings and is home to a roster of seasonal outdoor events including a July Moonlight Garden Party. The gardens are intermingled around a Sears & Roebuck barn, a one-room country schoolhouse, and restored buildings including a folly and wedding gazebo.

Specialties:
Seventy-five theme gardens entertain visitors who roam, wander, and explore all the plant offerings of Prairie Pedlar. A gift shop and greenhouse whet the gardener's appetite for herbs, one-of-a-kind container gardens, hanging baskets, hard-to-find perennials, and Proven Winners®.

Northwest Iowa

NW

Prairie Pedlar

What about favorite plant?
"I can't imagine having a country garden without the charm of a border of hollyhocks splashed up against the side of the barn," says Jane. But her list of favorites doesn't end there. "Autumn clematis is an amazing focal point when in bloom over the arbor in our fragrance garden." Still going she says "the border of Russian sage in the herb garden wows visitors from July through frost."

NW Rhoadside Blooming House
John & Donna Beier
205 Indian Street
Cherokee, IA 51012 *Cherokee*
712-225-5711
jdbeier@iowatelecom.net
www.rhoadsidebloominghouse.com

When are they there? Year-round. Monday-Friday, Saturday.
What are their hours? 8:00 AM to 5:00 PM, 8:00 AM to 3:00 PM

Specialties:
A visit to Rhoadside Blooming House will find quality home-grown annuals and perennials. Crops like cyclamen and poinsettias are also produced in-season at the holidays. Fresh flower arrangements, silks, houseplants, and statuary are also available in the gift shop.

Riveland Nursery & Garden Center
Larry & Cindy Riveland
10738 Falcon Avenue
Monona, IA 52159 *Monona*
563-539-2084
riveland@netins.net

When are they there? Year-round. Monday-Saturday, Sunday.
What are their hours? 8:00 AM to 6:00 PM, noon to 5:00 PM.

Specialties:
Riveland offers over 300 varieties of trees and shrubs and over 300 varieties of perennials, all of which you can see utilized in a series of display gardens around the property. Larry and Cindy aren't kidding when they say "you're sure to see something you like."

Northwest Iowa

NW

Saxton's Greenhouse & Floral
Paul Saxton
2103 19th St.
Emmetsburg, IA 50536 *Palo Alto*
712-852-4855
saxtons@emmetsburggreenhouse.com
www.emmetsburggreenhouse.com

When are they there? Year-round. Monday-Friday, Saturday.
What are their hours? 8:00 AM to 5:30 PM, 8:00 AM to 4:00 PM.

Specialties:
Saxton's specializes in larger-size geraniums, many cultivars of vegetative annuals, and mixed container combinations and hanging baskets. They are also Emmetsburg's premier florist and their full-service flower shop is open year-round.

The Squirrel's Nest, Inc.
Tracy Bosshart
702 E. Lincolnway
Jefferson, IA 50129 *Greene*
515-386-4042
squirrelsnest@netins.net

When are they there? Year-round. Monday-Saturday.
What are their hours? 10:00 AM to 5:00 PM.

Get to know them:
The Squirrel's Nest is located on the property known locally as Quirk's Cabins. It used to be an old motel on old Highway 30. There were 17 cabins, a bath house, and a restaurant on-site. The cabins have since been removed but the charm and lore of the former life of the site remains.

Specialties:
The Squirrel's Nest is known for their knowledgeable staff. They'll guide you through rows of unusual perennials, annuals, and gift baskets. Iowa wines, herbal products, and other gifts are also for sale.

What about favorite plant?
Cardinal climber. "It is very easy to grow," says Tracy noting its penchant for climbing over anything. "The hummers just love those red flowers too."

NW

Thistle Down Nursery
David and Michelle Witte
3045 Rolf Avenue
Lake View, IA 51450 *Sac*
712-662-4278
thsldwn@netins.net
http://tdnursery.com

When are they there? Seasonally and by appointment. Monday-Saturday, Sunday.
What are their hours? 8:00 AM to 5:00 PM, 1:00 PM to 4:00 PM.

Get to know them:
Thistle Down Nursery began on a vacant acreage lot that happened to be full of thistles (hence the name). The first greenhouse was built on top of the last thistle patch and was open to the public on the honor system, since both David and Michelle had full-time jobs. This charming little nursery offers hundreds of different plants and strives to keep a selection of unusual items in stock.

Specialties:
Thistle Down carries 500 varieties of perennials and a huge variety of hanging baskets. Custom order containers are also available. For unusual things they offer a number of carnivorous plants and some of their favorite not-often-seen annuals.

What about favorite plant?
When asked about their favorite plant Michelle replied with "that's like asking 'who's your favorite child?'" But in the end she settled on *Ligularia*. Oh and blue hostas too. "I love the bright yellow spikes of *Ligularia* against the huge dark leaves," says Michelle. "And hostas are the perfect shade plant."

Toft Tree Farm & Landscape Center
Gary Toft
2506 11 Avenue SW
Spencer, IA 51301 *Clay*
712-264-1102
jodie@smunet.net

When are they there? Seasonally. Spring. Monday-Sunday.
What are their hours? 8:00 AM to 6:00 PM.

Specialties:
At Toft Tree Farm and Landscape Center you'll find a variety of woody ornamentals including Proven Winners® shrubs and Endless Summer® hydrangeas. You'll also find Plantskydd® deer repellent and fertilizer products there too.

Northwest Iowa

NW

Tulip Town Bulb Co.
Brett & Nora Mulder
116 1st Street SW
Orange City, IA 51041 *Sioux*
712-737-3670
mulders@tuliptownbulbs.com
www.tuliptownbulbs.com

When are they there? Seasonally. Tulip bloom season.
What are their hours? Call for hours.

Get to know them:
Tulip Town Bulb Company was established in 2007, a reincarnated version of Vander Wel Tulip Test Gardens. The corner that the gardens are located on is the former location of a church which was later used as Northwestern College's theater department. The church building was razed in 2007. The display gardens on-site feature over 50 different varieties of tulips, totaling nearly 3,000 plants.

Specialties:
Tulips can be purchased on-site for mail-order delivery or pick-up. Orders are also taken from their website and shipped all over the country.

What about favorite plant?
A tulip cultivar called 'Charmeur' is a favorite of Brett and Nora because of the beautiful red-tipped white.

Northwest Iowa

NW

Other Places of Interest in the NW Iowa Region

Better Homes Nursery & Gardens
3800 Stone Park Boulevard
Sioux City, IA 51103 *Woodbury*

Correctionville Nursery
4161 150th Street
Correctionville, IA 51016 *Woodbury*

Cottage Gardener
Stephen A. Braddock
P.O. Box 423, 107 5th Street North
Swea City, IA 50590 *Kossuth*
515-272-4569
cottagegardener@hotmail.com

Country Gardens
303 Highway 71
Early, IA 50535 *Sac*

Country Side Gardens
2862 310th Street
Rock Valley, IA 51247 *Sioux*

Del's Garden Center, Inc.
Del & Todd Brockshus
1808 11th Street SE
Spencer, IA 51301 *Clay*
800-359-1416
www.delsgardencenter.com

Ferguson's Landscape & Garden Center
3602 Highway 715
Spirit Lake, IA 51360 *Dickinson*

Flower Barn
1439 1120th Street
Harlan, IA 51537 *Shelby*

Garden of Dreams
907 Market Street
Gowrie, IA 50543 *Webster*
515-352-3414

Garden's Gate
Twylla Baker
P.O. Box 552, 1309 North Main
Algona, IA 50511 *Kossuth*
515-295-8803
twyllab@earthlink.net

Goins Garden Center
701 West Franklin Street
Lake City, IA 51449 *Calhoun*
712-464-7638

Grube Lawn & Garden
112 2nd Street SW
Cresco, IA 51236 *Howard*
563-547-4835

Northwest Iowa

NW

Hiway Nursery & Landscaping
Randall Brinkman
149 North Highway 60, P.O. Box 346
Sheldon, IA 51201 *O'Brien*
712-324-4408

Jane's Green Thumb
Jane Houchins
105 Broadway Street
Exira, IA 50076 *Audobon*
712-268-2112
janethedane@yahoo.com

Jones Nursery & Garden Store
861 Highway 7
Storm Lake, IA 50588 *Buena Vista*
712-732-6785

Lunzman Nursery
2531 Jasper Avenue
Ida Grove, IA 51445 *Ida*
712-364-2002

Midwest Nursery, Inc.
1513 2nd Avenue
Sheldon, IA 51201 *O'Brien*

Mosher Garden Center
Paul & Mary Mosher
3235 Business 75 N
Sioux City, IA 51108 *Woodbury*
712-293-1333

Nelson's Nursery
304 West 4th Street
Auburn, IA 51433 *Sac*
712-688-2350

Oaks Garden Spot &
Rasmussen Lawn Care
Rick Rasmussen
707 Third Avenue South
P.O. Box 237
Dakota City, IA 50529 *Humboldt*
515-332-1778

Schmitz Nursery
2122 180th Street
Audubon, IA 50025 *Audubon*
712-563-3544

Silver Creek Nursery
30962 380th Street
Shelby, IA 51570 *Shelby*

Steburg's Nursery
3057 Highway 44
Panora, IA 50216 *Guthrie*
641-755-2969

Northwest Iowa

Three Oaks Greenhouse
Floral & Gift
Steve E. Peterson
704 W. Main St.
Lake Mills, IA 50450 *Winnebago*
888-833-6257
www.threeoaksgreenhouse.com

Willow Nursery & Garden Center
600 Montague Street
Dunlap, IA 51529 *Harrison*

Windy Ridge Flowers &
Willow Furniture
Gloria Brouse
1269 Fig Ave.
Coon Rapids, IA 50058 *Carroll*
712-684-5285

NW

Your Day Trip Planner for *Northwest Iowa*

I can't think of any gardener who wouldn't want to steal away at least one day in spring with a band of co-horts to take in sites of horticultural interest. But where to go can be a most vexing question with so many gardens and so little time. That's why I've composed the following day trip planner to assist you in your preparations for a day afield enjoying the bounty of Iowa's garden attractions. Though you're certainly free to put your own together, I thought you might enjoy this trip that I took once.

Best time of year: Spring
Estimated round-trip mileage: 150 miles
Number of places: 3

I've been going to **The Prairie Pedlar** of rural Odebolt since I was a teenager. This family endeavor settled between tall rows of popcorn fields has grown from humble beginnings to become a treasured destination of many gardeners. Hosting various themed festivals and galas throughout the growing season, owners and hosts Jack and Jane Hogue invite gardeners from near and far to enjoy their vintage Sears and Roebuck barn and buildings and most lovely gardens. Jane is fond of herbs too so it shouldn't be a surprise to find collections of everything from basil to scented geraniums. If you don't come away inspired and with arms full of plants, you didn't make it there in the first place. I'll let you be the judge of their containers and hanging baskets too. Also, if you make it on a festival day, you can enjoy home-cooked lunch on site.

Northwest Iowa

NW

Heading east you can't help but veer the car to the north just outside of Lake View to check in on **Thistle Down Nursery**. The theme of this trip is personality and each step has a unique ambiance to share with their clients. While The Prairie Pedlar offers you the chance to stroll in a countryside garden, Thistle Down Nursery will wow you by the hundreds of varieties of plants they carry. If you're on the hunt for heirloom tomatoes today, you'll find them reasonably priced here.

After a morning of nurseries in a rural setting, why not get lost in a garden center in Carroll? At least that's how **Enchanted Gardens** bills itself, and it's not a shallow assessment either. The dream project of owner Gina Bauck, this retreat lets visitors feel relaxed in a sales-oriented environment. If you've not found a container yet that's caught your eye, this will be your last chance!

Northeast Iowa

Northeast Iowa may well win the prize for density and diversity. There are nurseries and garden centers everywhere! I once heard that to embark on a trip to northeast Iowa required heading for the hills, a most obvious conclusion if you had an altimeter handy.

But the small rise in elevation won't be noticed once you've found a few of these places, some of which are the best known in the state. Mention northeast Iowa in many well-buffed gardening circles and most can recite two to three names easily. It's what happens when gardeners travel -- they tell their friends.

Literature has also exploited the beauty of Northeast Iowa. After all, to many our state is not known as the Hawkeye state but instead a field of dreams. Children's books have told of the mysteries of Backbone State Park and historical works have documented the prestige and ancient charm of the Effigy Mounds.

A trip to northeast Iowa can enthrall the whole family. Take one bunch to a few nurseries, let another explore the geography, and meet up for a ride down the river, falls and all. Whatever the way, it's well worth a visit.

Northeast Iowa

NE

7 Bluffs Landscaping & Nursery
Cheryl Whalen
11390 North Cascade Road
Dubuque, IA 52003 *Dubuque*
563-588-2334

When are they there? Seasonally. May-June. Monday-Friday, Saturday-Sunday.
What are their hours? 9:00 AM to 7:00 PM, 9:00 AM to 4:00 PM

Get to know them:
The business is located in a renovated 1913 round tile barn with the retail operation located on the first floor and apartments on the second and third floors.

Specialties:
In addition to landscape design services, a large retail nursery features perennials, evergreens, flowering shrubs, shade trees, and ornamental grasses. Outdoor garden features like fountains, bird baths, and statues are also on sale.

Annie's Gardens & Greens
Ann Bushman
30975 Lincoln Road
Fort Atkinson, IA 52144 *Winneshiek*
563-534-7760
nna_namhsub@yahoo.com

When are they there? Seasonally. Monday-Saturday
What are their hours? 8:00 AM to 6:00 PM

Get to know them:
Annie's Gardens & Greens specializes in herbs, a passion passed on by her grandmother. Ann's business has grown as she's continued to experiment with herbs. "I love growing them from seed to have the experience of knowing first hand," Ann says. She believes that herbs give you "a newfound respect for plants and their usefulness." Though only open seasonally, her herbal retreat is surely the place to visit in northeast Iowa if you're looking for a tangy spice or sweet aroma for your house or garden. A catalog and plant list are available.

Specialties:
Herbs and heirloom tomato plants for sale. Also available for purchase are dried herbs, herbal blends, herbal teas, and herbal oils. Grilling and tea workshops on the uses of herbs held during the growing season.

What about favorite plant?
Lovage. "My grandmother gave it to me and sparked my interest in herbs," says Ann. Lovage is known for its aromatic qualities and its use as a food flavoring.

Northeast Iowa

NE

Becky's Greenhouse
Becky Litterer
80 South Main Street
Doughtery, IA 50433 *Cerro Gordo*
641-794-3337
beckmail@netins.net

When are they there? Year-round. Monday-Sunday in May
What are their hours? Call for hours.

Get to know them:
Becky's Greenhouse is noted for her reasonable prices and knowledgeable staff. She sells perennials, annuals, vegetables, geraniums, roses, and hanging baskets. She also has seed potatoes, onion sets, and bulk seeds available for purchase. Don't forget the garden decorations too!

Specialties:
A full service greenhouse garden center offering a wide array of plants.

Northeast Iowa

Bickelhaupt Arboretum
Francie B. Hill
340 South 14th Street
Clinton, IA 52732 *Clinton*
563-242-4771
bickarb@clinton.net
www.bickarb.org

NE

Do they charge admission? No

When are they there? Year-round. Monday-Sunday
What are their hours? Dawn to dusk

Get to know them:
The Bickelhaupt Arboretum is a 14-acre outdoor museum that showcases one of the finest collections of dwarf conifers, trees, and shrubs in Iowa and the Midwest. A busy schedule of educational events and entertaining displays keeps something happening at this family project turned public garden. The arboretum was founded by Frances and Bob Bickelhaupt on the property surrounding their home and was given to the public in 1970. A complete plant list is available on-site at the Visitor's Center which houses local artifacts, native plant and animal displays, a library, and a meeting room.

Specialties:
Extensive plant collections and a commitment to fostering connections between people and plants through a better understanding of horticulture draws thousands of visitors to this must-see arboretum on a yearly basis.

What about favorite plant?
Executive Director Francie Hill remarks that her favorite plants are "any new witches' broom that shows up on a conifer. I like them because of their very unusual growths."

Northeast Iowa

NE

Bickelhaupt Arboretum

Northeast Iowa

NE

NE

Bird View Gardens
Jerry and Pat McHenry
1147 Highway 30
Montour, IA 50173 *Tama*
641-479-2408
pjmchenry@iowatelecom.net
www.birdviewgardens.com

Do they charge admission? No

When are they there? Seasonally. Monday-Sunday
What are their hours? 8:00 AM to 4:00 PM

Get to know them:
Bird View Gardens is the project Jerry & Pat McHenry who founded the garden in 1984. Open to the public seasonally, this certified National Wildlife Federation Backyard Wildlife Habitat is a sanctuary for gardeners and animals alike. Jerry and Pat have extensive collections of Buck roses, irises, daylilies, crabapples, and flowering shrubs. Nestled amongst 20 acres of old growth timber, Bird View Gardens attracts flocks of feathered friends each season including nesting wood ducks, bluebirds, wrens, and purple martins.

Specialties:
Award-winning wildlife sanctuary with appealing displays of flowering shrubs, trees, and fruiting plants.

What about favorite plant?
Arrowwood viburnum (*Viburnum dentatum*). "The berries ripen in fall just in time for the migrating birds," says Jerry and Pat. "We think this hard little berry wouldn't be very appealing but more species visit this shrub than any other in our collection."

Boots Nursery, Inc.
Anna Mary Riniker
707 East 2nd and 3rd Streets
Anamosa, IA 52205 *Jones*
319-462-2151
AMBoots@bdrcpa.com

When are they there? Seasonally. Monday-Saturday
What are their hours? 9:00 AM to 5:00 PM. Call for additional hours.

Get to know them:
This small town, family-run nursery was started 40 years ago by Anna Mary's mother. The operation is known for their extensive selection of bedding plants, vegetables, shrubs, flowering and fruit trees, as well as other ornamentals. "You have to like cats if you come here!" notes Anna Mary. A few pet rabbits are also not out of the question.

Specialties:
A full-service greenhouse garden center offering a wide array of plants, complete with kitties and rabbits.

What about favorite plant?
Geraniums (*Pelargonium*). "My mother started the greenhouse 40 years ago and has always had the deepest and most beautiful red geraniums for Memorial Day," says Anna Mary.

Northeast Iowa

NE

Brucemore Gardens
2160 Linden Drive SE
Cedar Rapids, IA 52403 *Linn*
319-362-7375
www.brucemore.org

Do they charge admission? Yes

When are they there? Year-round. Tuesday-Saturday, Sunday
What are their hours? 10:00 AM to 3:00 PM, 12:00 PM to 3:00 PM

Get to know them:
The 26-acre Brucemore Gardens are perhaps the most elegant gardens in Cedar Rapids. The gardens, fashioned as outdoor rooms, were designed by landscape architect O.C. Simonds in 1910 in the style of English country gardens. Today the gardens contain a colorful and exuberant collection of heirloom and new plants. Theme gardens include a formal garden, cutting garden, children's garden, woodland, and night garden. One of the few public gardens in the area, Brucemore is the perfect setting for outdoor recreation and leisure.

Specialties:
Theme gardens and a well-managed landscape offer the public of eastern Iowa access to one of the finest public landscapes in the state. Classical, elegant, and with an air of an olden day, Brucemore is a must see if you're in the Cedar Rapids area.

What about favorite plant?
Clematis. The staff of Brucemore is particularly fond of this classic vine. Coming in a variety of colors and textures, it provides visual interest from spring to fall. Clematis are used in containers throughout the estate and frequently incorporated into cut-flower arrangements at the Brucemore Cutting Gardens Flower Shop.

Northeast Iowa

NE

Cannon's Greenhouses
Darryl & Jane Cannon
345 Eastline Street North
Westgate, IA 50681 *Fayette*
563-578-8669

When are they there? Seasonally. Monday-Friday, Saturday, Sunday
What are their hours? 9:00 AM to 6:00 PM, 9:00 AM to 4:00 PM, 10:00 AM to 3:00 PM. Call for additional hours especially if you are coming from a distance.

Get to know them:
Cannon's Greenhouses is a small "mom and pop" business but carries a wide variety and great selection of plants. Four greenhouses are filled to the brim each spring with geraniums, hanging baskets, bedding plants and perennials. Two acres of trees and shrubs are available including a nice offering of sculptured evergreens. Darryl and Jane comment that they "have many regular customers from about an hour radius," understandably so with such a diverse inventory.

Specialties:
As their business card states "a full line of bedding plants, trees, and shrubs" with an emphasis on reasonable prices and selection.

What about favorite plant?
Geranium (*Pelargonium*) because of their versatility.

Northeast Iowa

NE

Chalupsky Landscaping & Nursery Inc.
Jim & Joan Chalupsky
1270 Curtis Bridge Road NE
Shueyville, IA 52338 *Johnson*
319-848-7402

When are they there? Seasonally. Monday-Sunday
What are their hours? 8:00 AM to 5:00 PM

Get to know them:
Jim and Joan Chalupsky say their nursery is great for browsing. Set in a quiet country setting, their nursery mingles with interesting and colorful gardens and water features. They offer bonsai, Iowa-grown trees, perennials, shrubs, evergreens, and roses. An added touch is a cutting garden for those who desire fresh flowers for their home or gifts. Joan says future plans for the nursery include adding a nature walk through the trees on their 28-acre property. "It will be a place for people to reflect on nature and enjoy some quiet time."

Specialties:
The three-acre nursery facility not only carries an excellent selection of plants but landscaping supplies as well. Jim and Joan have hired a knowledgeable staff that is able to assist you with the design and development of your garden.

What about favorite plant?
Jim and Joan's three favorite plants are bur oak (*Quercus macrocarpa*), azalea hybrids, and roses, each representing the groups of plants they produce: trees, shrubs, and flowers. Joan likes oaks for their stately habits, azaleas for their riots of colorful blooms, and roses for their lasting, fragrant flowers.

Northeast Iowa

NE

Corner Market & Greenhouse
Paul & Linda Manske
5851 Palace Road
Mailing address: 16395 50th Street
Oelwein, IA 50662 *Fayette*
319-283-1905
micasa@n-connect.net

When are they there? Seasonally. Monday-Saturday, Sunday, Easter through Christmas.
What are their hours? 9:00 AM to 5:00 PM, 10:00 AM to 5:00 PM

Get to know them:
Paul and Linda Manske's operation showcases the largest selection of statuary and garden ornaments in northeast Iowa. Boasting everything from hand-tuned wind chimes and gazing balls to fountains and street lamp posts, you'll surely find something to decorate your garden with at Corner Market & Greenhouse. They also carry unique varieties of annuals and perennials, hanging baskets, combination planters, and garden vegetables. A popular service is their custom Memorial Day planters. You provide the pot and they'll plant it for you.

Specialties:
This northeast Iowa garden shop is a year-round source of everything a gardener needs, from plants in spring, produce in summer, and Christmas decorations during the holidays.

What about favorite plant?
Coleus (*Solenostemon*). "They come in hundreds of colors, work in sun or shade, and can be compact or tall," says Paul and Linda. "They make beautiful landscape and container combinations, look good just about everywhere, and provide such great contrasts."

Northeast Iowa

NE Culver's Garden Center & Greenhouse
Todd & Tami Culver
1682 Dubuque Rd.
Marion, IA 52302 *Linn*
319-377-4195
www.culverslandscape.com

When are they there? Year-round. Call for open days.
What are their hours? Call for open hours.

Get to know them:
The easily accessed Culver's Garden Center is situated on 27 acres right off of Highway 151. Started in 1998 as an extension of Culver's Lawn Care and Landscaping, Inc., the trendy garden center features home and garden decor and 14 greenhouses of plant products. In addition to this they also offer complete residential and commercial landscaping services, lawn care and maintenance, pond installation and more.

Specialties:
Culver's is known for what it calls "bigger blooming, better performing" plants. Their extensive landscape nursery should fulfill most gardener's plant

wants and needs. The latest outdoor living decor can be found inside when you've finished perusing the extensive offering of plants.

Dubuque Arboretum & Botanical Gardens
Jack Frick, President
3800 Arboretum Drive
Dubuque, IA 52001 *Dubuque*
563-556-2100
DubArbBotGardens@aol.com
www.idbq.com/arboretum

Do they charge admission? No

When are they there? Year-round. Daily.
What are their hours? 7:00 AM to Dusk.

Get to know them:
My first visit to the Dubuque Arboretum and Botanical Garden was 11 years ago at the tender age of 10. This garden is perhaps the best in our state and is solely maintained by the arduous efforts of 280 volunteers. Tucked away in the hills of north Dubuque, this botanical gem features renowned hosta and dwarf conifer collections. But particularly enjoyable is the atmosphere of civic involvement warmed by the sounds of music piped throughout the garden. A visit to the garden in June will get you in during a jaw-dropping rose display. If you haven't visited you're missing out.

Specialties:
Garden exhibits at the Arboretum include the newly constructed Japanese garden, world's largest public hosta garden, All-America Rose Selections garden, dwarf conifer collection, and many beds of perennials and annuals.

What about favorite plant?
President Jack Frick is the man in-charge and can be found at the Arboretum on a daily basis. When asked what his favorite plant was he couldn't help but pick tea roses. "They're just beautiful and sometimes you even get a great smell."

Northeast Iowa

NE

Fort Atkinson Nursery
Steven Sindelar
400 1st Street NW
Fort Atkinson, IA 52144 *Winneshiek*
563-534-7273
bosco3@acegroup.cc

When are they there? Seasonally. April-June. Monday-Saturday, Sunday.
What are their hours? 8:00 AM to 5:00 PM, 1:00 PM to 5:00 PM.

Specialties:
Fort Atkinson Nursery is a source for 'Tauntoni' spreading yew, dwarf trees, dawn redwoods, grafted dwarf fruit trees, and the landscaped property around the nursery.

Northeast Iowa

Fran Mara Gardens
Gary & Tom Whittenbaugh
625 Third Avenue SW
Oelwein, IA 50662 *Fayette*
franmara@trxinc.com

NE

Do they charge admission? No

When are they there? By appointment.
What are their hours? Email for an appointment.

Get to know them:
Fran Mara Gardens is the life work of Gary Whittenbaugh and his brother Tom. This collection of dwarf conifers and alpine plants is highly regarded as one of the best in the Midwest. Packed into a 70 x 150 lot, visitors enter another world when perusing the rock gardens that the two brothers have created around their family home.

Specialties:
Dwarf conifers are the mantra here. Alpines and companion perennials for dwarf conifers are also showcased but are always secondary to the trees!

What about favorite plant?
Gary's cheeky and oft-heard answer: "Whatever I happen to be standing in front of at the moment."

Northeast Iowa

NE

Happy Acres Nursery
Mary & Jerry Fisk
2012 Highway 9
Osage, IA 50461 *Mitchell*
641-732-5173
jfisk@osage.net

When are they there? Year-round. Monday-Saturday, Sunday.
What are their hours? 8:30 AM to 5:30 PM, 11:00 AM to 4:00 PM

Get to know them:
Happy Acres has been in business for 26 years helping visitors find the right plants for their outdoor living spaces. The complete garden center is located in a wooded setting and aims to offer customers new and different plants. Both Mary and Jerry are Master Gardeners and happy to answer your gardening questions.

Specialties:
Happy Acres offers a vast selection of trees, shrubs, perennials, and annuals. They also offer landscape design and installation services, including retaining walls and other hardscapes.

What about favorite plant?
Any hosta.

Harris Greenhouse & Garden Center
Mary Longfellow
807 7th Street
Belle Plaine, IA 55208 *Benton*
319-444-3001
mlongfellow@mchsi.com
www.harrisgreenhouse.com

When are they there? Seasonally. Monday-Saturday, Sunday.
What are their hours? 9:00 AM to 5:00 PM, 12:00 PM to 5:00 PM.

Get to know them:
This family-owned business has had its doors open since 1964. You'll find six greenhouses at this small-town business as well as a friendly atmosphere and comfortable buying environment.

Specialties:
Mary carries a wide variety of products including bedding plants, Proven Winners® products, shrubs, and hanging baskets.

What about favorite plant?
Black-eyed Susan.

Northeast Iowa

NE

Heavenly Hostas, Ornamental Grasses, & Perennials
Lynn Farmer
1518 Forest Grove Rd.
Cedar Rapids, IA 52403 *Linn*
319-361-9256
lfarmer27@mchsi.com

When are they there? Seasonally and by appointment.
What are their hours? Call for open hours.

Specialties:
You'll find hostas, ornamental grasses, daylilies, bearded irises, Siberian irises, and more here.

Horak's Landscape Nursery
Richard Horak
1354 Curtis Bridge Road NE
Swisher, IA 52338 *Johnson*
319-848-7222

When are they there? Seasonally and by appointment. April-June. Monday-Saturday.
What are their hours? 9:00 AM to 1:00 PM

Get to know them:
Horak's Landscape Nursery started in 1972 with a few rows of tree seedlings. It's grown into an 11-acre nursery filled with nostalgic, horse-drawn equipment, a sharp contrast to modern tree spades used today. The nursery residence was pulled down the road from two miles away using tree bags for wheels in the late 1800s. The newest addition was built in 1907. Owner Richard Horak says they thoroughly test cultivars over many years before offering them for sale. "This way we insure our local customers that they are getting reliable plants for our climate zone."

Specialties:
Horak's carries many evergreens and deciduous trees including their own selections of red maple, American arborvitae, black raspberry, and purple leaf ash.

What about favorite plant?
Richard says he likes the larger arborvitaes. "They are so friendly, easy-to-grow and transplant, not spiny, have few disease and pest problems, and provide a peaceful privacy."

NE

In the Country Garden & Gifts
Josh & Sue Spece
2392 240th St.
Independence, IA 50644 *Buchanan*
319-334-6593
josh@inthecountrygardenandgifts.com
www.inthecountrygardenandgifts.com

When are they there? Seasonally and by appointment. Tuesday-Sunday.
What are their hours? 9:00 AM to 6:00 PM

Get to know them:
Started in 1998 by mother-and-son duo Sue and Josh Spece, In the Country Garden & Gifts has grown to become the largest source of aquatic plants in northeast Iowa. In addition to the nursery, Sue's creative knack has resulted in a delightful gift shop full of homespun gifts and unique garden decor. Josh is active in many plant societies and writes on topics ranging from water gardening to hostas. Recently the Speces have added a line of heirloom annuals and vegetables encouraged by Sue's son-in-law Jim Heinz.

Specialties:
Josh and Sue offer over 400 collector hostas, shade companion plants, water plants, and supplies to fit your yard with a great water garden. Rock garden plants and succulents are also available.

What about favorite plant?
Josh is obviously fond of hostas. He likes that they are easy-to-grow and come in a huge variety of colors, sizes, shapes, textures, and personalities.

Northeast Iowa

Ingrid's Landscaping
Ingrid C. Anderson-Quint
210 Adams Street
Ryan, IA 52330 *Delaware*
563-932-2990

NE

When are they there? By appointment only.
What are their hours? Call to schedule an appointment.

Get to know them:
The nursery is primarily associated with Ingrid's landscape installation work. The nursery is very small and is only open by appointment.

65

Northeast Iowa

NE

Jim's Hostas
Jim Schwarz
11616 Robin Hood
Dubuque, IA 52001 *Dubuque*
563-588-9671
jschw94560@aol.com
www.jimshostas.com

When are they there? By appointment only.
What are their hours? Call for an appointment.

Get to know them:
Jim's collection of hostas is one of the largest in the country with over 2,700 cultivars growing and for sale in his three acre backyard. He has introduced a number of his own cultivars all of which tend to be named with a Robin Hood theme (he lives on Robin Hood Drive after all). Jim's Hostas is primarily a mail-order business with sales taken from their website. On-site visitors are accommodated by appointment only. A print catalog is available for two first-class stamps.

Specialties:
2,700 varieties of hostas will overwhelm you. Now that's a specialty!

What about favorite plant?
Do you even have to ask?

K & K Gardens
Keith & Kelli Kovarik
108 East Wilbur Street
Hawkeye, IA 52147 *Fayette*
563-427-5373
kkgardens@netins.net
www.kkgardens.com

NE

When are they there? Seasonally. May 1st-September 30th. Sunday-Saturday.
What are their hours? Check website for current season's hours.

Get to know them:
Keith and Kelli started K & K Gardens as hobby in 1995. "It has grown leaps and bounds since then," says Keith. While both maintain full-time jobs away from the nursery, they still find time to operate their innovative retail garden center in their residential neighborhood. "Many refer to our place as a 'must-see destination nursery'. People have fun and always bring many more people back time and time again," says Keith of his gardens.

Specialties:
Keith and Kelli specialize in water gardens but have several display gardens that meander throughout their property. Unusual annuals and perennials and woody ornamentals can be found at this nursery in addition to pond plants, supplies, and garden gifts.

What about favorite plant?
Ligularia 'The Rocket' ranks especially high with Keith and Kelli. "Really I just think the name is cool!" remarks Keith. He cites its easy going, good personality and showy nature as reasons why he likes it.

Northeast Iowa

NE

Krieger's Greenhouse & Floral
2299 4th St. SE
Mason City, IA 50401 *Cerro Gordo*
641-424-2307
kriegersgreenhouse@yahoo.com

When are they there? Year-round. Monday-Saturday.
What are their hours? 8:30 AM to 5:00 PM

Get to know them:
This family-owned business was started in 1890 and is now in its fifth generation. Krieger's has both an active wholesale and retail business providing bedding plants, houseplants, holiday plants, and gardening supplies to gardeners and growers all over the Midwest. During the summer they have a vegetable market too.

Specialties:
Krieger's pride is that it produces all of the plants it sells. In addition to bedding plants and other seasonal plants (including poinsettias at Christmas), they also operate a full-service floral shop.

What about favorite plant?
Karen Krieger's favorite plants are poinsettia and impatiens. Both, she says, are beautiful and carefree.

Northeast Iowa

NE

Otto's Oasis
Jeff & Lori Otto
1313 Gilbert Street
Charles City, IA 50616 *Floyd*
641-228-6193
ghouse@fa.net
www.ottosoasis.com

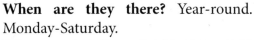

When are they there? Year-round. Monday-Saturday.
What are their hours? 8:00 AM to 5:30 PM

Get to know them:
Otto's Oasis is a family-owned and -operated business that has been serving the Charles City area since 1989. Jeff and Lori took over the family business in 2007 and continue to offer the finest floral arrangements year-round. The business is also known for its expansive garden center.

Specialties:
Otto's supplies gardeners in the area with annuals, perennials, geraniums, and tropicals. Visitors will be delighted at the great and excellently priced selection. Iowa wines are also available in the gift area.

What about favorite plant?
Dipladenia (*Mandevilla splendens*). "It's a popular favorite in our store because it withstands heat and wind," says Lori.

69

Northeast Iowa

NE

Ridge Road Nursery
Eugene W. Coffman
3025 St. Catherine Road
Bellevue, IA 52031 *Jackson*
563-583-1381
ewcoff@earthlink.com
www.ridgeroadplants.com

When are they there? Call for an appointment.

What are their hours? Call for hours.

Get to know them:
Eugene "Doc" Coffman was a doctor of internal medicine in a former life. In retirement he has gained regard as of the more acute plantsmen of the Midwest. While the nursery is run by his business partner Chris Frommelt, an able landscaper herself, Doc's charming and enlivening presence embodies the spirit of the nursery on a daily basis. Always on the lookout for an unusual plant, Doc can spend hours telling you stories about his more than 25 years of experiences with plants.

Specialties:
The nursery is mainly a landscape nursery offering field and container grown trees and shrubs in larger sizes for commercial and residential projects.

What about favorite plant?
I'm sure Doc can share "a few" with you when you stop by.

Northeast Iowa

NE

NE **Riverside Gardens**
Judy Tuetken
441 East Third Street
Monticello, IA 52310 *Jones*
319-465-5626
chamber@macc.ia.us
www.macc-ia.us

Do they charge admission? No

When are they there? Year-round. Monday-Sunday.
What are their hours? 4:00 AM to 10:00 PM

Get to know them:
Riverside Gardens is a Jones County treasure prized for its wonderful flower displays open to the public free of charge. The gardens showcase perennials and annuals in 30 beds that are complemented by picnic areas, a gazebo, wishing well, nature trails, and a wetlands area. The public park is popular for gatherings and events. Funding for the garden is provided for by the sale of postcards of the picturesque displays.

Specialties:
This public garden offers gardeners ideas to implement in country-style gardens.

Northeast Iowa

NE

Scotch Grove Nursery
Janette Bohlken
16336 116th Avenue
Scotch Grove, IA 52310 *Jones*
319-465-3985

When are they there? Seasonally. Monday-Saturday, Sunday.
What are their hours? 8:00 AM to 5:00 PM, 1:00 PM to 4:00 PM.

Specialties:
Scotch Grove carries grown-on-site windbreak trees, shade, fruit, and ornamental trees hardy to the area, and flowering shrubs and roses. Perennials, small fruits, and daylilies are also for sale.

NE

Steve's Ace Home & Garden
Judy and Steve Selchert
3350 John F. Kennedy Road
Dubuque, IA 52002 *Dubuque*
563-690-1500
j.selchert@gmail.com

When are they there? Call for open days.
What are their hours? Call for open hours.

Get to know them:
Steve's Ace Home and Garden Center is one of the best-merchandised garden centers in the tri-state area. Dubuque residents no doubt rank this as a local prize. They also operate a full-service floral shop with the ability to send flowers worldwide, all from their hardware store.

Specialties:
You'll find shrubs, annuals, perennials, trees, and vegetables at this expansive garden center. A recent addition to the business is power equipment sales and service.

What about favorite plant?
Steve and Judy are partial to 'Gentsch White' hemlock. "It's a shade-loving evergreen that isn't seen a lot," they say. "Plus cuttings of it make for great color in winter containers."

Stillwater Greenhouse
Daniel & Reba Zimmerman
3110 Shadow Avenue
Orchard, IA 50460 *Mitchell*
641-732-3252

When are they there? Seasonally. April-June. Monday-Saturday.
What are their hours? 8:00 AM to 8:00 PM.

Get to know them:
In 2000, Daniel built Reba a 700-square foot greenhouse for her own gardening use. By spring, though, it was busting at the seams so they advertised to get rid of the excess and the rest is history. Stillwater Greenhouse now has 25,000 square feet of production space for annuals and perennials and additional outdoor production space for trees and shrubs. See here for yourself what a hobby can truly become!

Specialties:
Stillwater carries what they call "one of the largest selection of annuals in the state." Combination baskets and patio containers are also for sale in addition to the newest perennials and shrubs.

What about favorite plant?
"We've become fond of 'Supertunia Vista Bubblegum' petunia from Proven Winners®. It's the most aggressive petunia on the market," says Daniel.

NE Sue's Flower & Garden Center
Susan Broghammer
1146 N. Franklin St.
Manchester, IA 52057 *Delaware*
563-927-6046

When are they there? Year-round. Monday-Friday, Saturday.
What are their hours? 9:00 AM to 5:00 PM, 9:00 AM to 4:00 PM.

Specialties:
"We carry a huge variety of bedding plants and zonal geraniums," says owner Susan Broghammer. You'll also find trees, shrubs, and perennials in the garden center plus houseplants in the floral shop. Thousands of decorations at Christmas time are an added find.

The Hosta Leaf
Bob & Julie Hackbarth
3016 115th Street
Colesburg, IA 52035 *Delaware*
563-856-3595
hostaleaf@iowatelecom.net

When are they there? Seasonally and by appointment. May-June. Saturday-Sunday.
What are their hours? 10:00 AM to 5:00 PM.

Get to know them:
The Hosta Leaf is a family owned and operated business. A typical visit to The Hosta Leaf begins by taking a leisurely walk through the numerous display beds that Bob and Tyler Hackbarth have created. The display areas feature 3 ponds, approximately 2000 varieties of hostas, numerous other perennials, and an amazing view of the surrounding countryside. Next, you can step inside an old grainary building that has been converted into a gift shop called The Potting Shed.

Specialties:
Hostas, garden gifts, and other shade perennials can be found at The Hosta Leaf.

What about favorite plant?
Judy says that "Hostas are fun to grow, they are almost maintenance free, very appealing in the landscape, and they are a plant that both women and men love to collect & grow."

NE

The Perennial Flower Farm
Steve & Caroline Bertrand
3036 Gilmore Ave.
Ionia, IA 50645 *Chickasaw*
641-435-4070
tpff@fiai.net

When are they there? Seasonally and by appointment. May 1-October 1. Wednesday-Saturday, Sunday.
What are their hours? 10:00 AM to 7:00 PM, 11:00 AM to 3:00 PM.

Get to know them:
The Perennial Flower Farm has been in business for over 20 years and has been operated by the plantsmen duo of Steve and Caroline Bertrand. The Bertrands specialize in plants that you'll be hard-pressed to find at probably any other nursery in the state. Full of knowledge, they can help advanced gardeners choose plants for rock gardens, shady borders, and just about any place you'd want to put a plant.

Specialties:
The Perennial Flower Farm has become known for quality garden perennials. The specialize in seed-propagated alpine

plants and bulbs while also carrying a number of lilies, all of which have been selected and propagated on-site.

What about favorite plant?
Steve and Caroline are reluctant to pick favorites. Everything they grow is a favorite!

Northeast Iowa

NE

Northeast Iowa

NE

Willowglen Nursery
Lee Zieke & Lindsay Lee
3512 Lost Mile Road
Decorah, IA 52101 *Winneshiek*
563-735-5570
www.willowglennursery.com

When are they there? Seasonally. May 1-September 30. Tuesday-Sunday.
What are their hours? 10:00 AM to 6:00 PM.

Get to know them:
Willowglen is a destination perennial flower nursery located in the hills of northeast Iowa. Lee and Lindsay are always doing something interesting with plants. They maintain a collection of willow that Lee uses for her basketry and that Lindsay finds uses for in the gardens and his craft projects. A large display garden is also found behind the nursery where visitors can see dynamic combinations of perennials in action.

Specialties:
Willowglen carries over 600 varieties of perennials that will surely entice any visitor. Don't be afraid to pick Lindsay's brain about design ideas. He's very talented in this area.

What about favorite plant?
Lee is partial to verbascums and sanguisorbas, a number of which you can find in their display gardens and for sale at their nursery.

Northeast Iowa

NE

Northeast Iowa

NE   **Willowglen Nursery**

Northeast Iowa

NE

Other Places of Interest in the NE Iowa Region

Andresen Landscaping & Garden Center
Bill Andresen
2826 234th Street
DeWitt, IA 52742 *Clinton*
563-659-5321

Basswood Gardens
23506 Basswood Avenue
Elgin, IA 52141 *Fayette*
563-245-2343

Bear Creek Landscapes & Nursery
3185 Union Road
Cedar Falls, IA 50613 *Black Hawk*
319-277-6643

Belle Plaine Nursery
506 4th Avenue, P.O. Box 137
Belle Plaine, IA 52208 *Benton*
888-202-2762

Blooming Acres
1170 1st Ave North
Mount Vernon, IA 52314 *Linn*
319-895-6077

Brocka Gardens Inc.
2464 Joplin Avenue
Denver, IA 50622 *Bremer*
319-984-9195

Cedar River Garden Center
2889 Palo Marsh Road
Palo, IA 52324 *Linn*
319-351-2161
http://www.cedarrivergardencenter.com/

Cedar Valley Botanic Gardens
1927 East Orange Road
Waterloo, IA 50704 *Black Hawk*
319-226-4966

Chick-A-Dee Garden
308 Main Street
Nashua, IA 50658 *Chickasaw*
641-435-2444

Dawn's Bloomers
1675 Golf Course Boulevard #23
Independence, IA 50644 *Buchanan*
319-334-3602
http://dajbloomer.googlepages.com/

Northeast Iowa

NE

Deutmeyer Nursery & Sod
Thomas Deutmeyer
1302 8th Avenue SE
Dyersville, IA 52040 *Dubuque*
563-875-8535
deutnursery@mwci.net

Dobie's Flowers
18722 Durango Rd.
Durango, IA 52039 *Dubuque*
563-552-1907

Dusty Roads Greenhouse
1548 300th Street
Nashua, IA 50658 *Chickasaw*
641-435-2592

Fairfax Greenhouses
PO Box 159
Fairfax, IA 52228 *Linn*

Fox Ridge Herbs
Julie Ladd
4918 Red School Rd.
Central City, IA 52214 *Linn*
319-438-6687

Henzler's Garden Shop
P.O. Box 93
Decorah, IA 52101 *Winneshiek*
563-382-5545

Hermsen Nursery
11431 Jamesmeier Road
Farley, IA 52046 *Dubuque*
563-744-3991

Hershey Family Nursery
27898 Douglas Avenue
Ackley, IA 50601 *Franklin*
http://hersheyfamilynursery.tripod.com

Ion Exchange
Howard Bright
1878 Old Mission Drive
Harpers Ferry, IA 52146 *Allamakee*
800-291-2143

Northeast Iowa

NE

Jolene S Flower Farm
1198 210th Street
Waverly, IA 50677 *Bremer*

Jordan's Nursery
Dan Jordan
1715 West 1st St., P.O. Box 484
Cedar Falls, IA 50613 *Black Hawk*
319-266-4717

Meyers Nursery
1685 Independence Avenue
Waterloo, IA 50707 *Black Hawk*
319-232-3954
meyersnursery@aol.com

Noelridge Park
4900 Council St. NE
Cedar Rapids, IA 52402 *Linn*
319-286-5753

Norwegian Nursery & Landscapes
5111 Twin Mound Drive NE
Cedar Rapids, IA 52402 *Linn*
319-395-7115

Our Tara Nursery & Garden Center
1231 Highway 9
Lansing, IA 52151 *Allamakee*
563-568-2665

Peck's Green Thumb Nursery
Kenneth & Shirley Peckosh
3990 Blairs Ferry Rd. NE
Cedar Rapids, IA 52402 *Linn*
319-393-5946

Pierson's Flower Shop &
Greenhouses
1800 Ellis Blvd. NW
Cedar Rapids, IA 52405 *Linn*
319-366-1826

Platt's Nursery Garden Shop
3700 University Avenue
Waterloo, IA 50701 *Black Hawk*
319-234-2686

Prairie Creek Nursery
4100 Bowling St. SW
Cedar Rapids, IA 52404 *Linn*
319-365-1406
Kevin@prairiecreeknursery.com
www.prairiecreeknursery.com

Seed Savers Exchange
3076 North Winn Road
Decorah, IA 52101 *Winneshiek*
563-382-5990
www.seedsavers.org

Northeast Iowa

NE

Splendid Valley Nursery
15071 Route # 20
Peosta, IA 52068 *Dubuque*
319-557-8325

The Peony Garden
Elvin Mackerman
95 Franklin Street
Center Point, IA 52213 *Linn*
319-849-1516
mr_mac_33@yahoo.com
www.peonygarden.net

The Plant Peddler
Mike Gooder
5302 2nd Avenue SW
Cresco, IA 52136 *Howard*

Valley View Nursery Landscape
3142 Feather Ridge Road
Toddville, IA 52341 *Linn*

Wagner Nursery, Inc
Doug Wagner
2677 Hales Mill Road
Dubuque, IA 52002 *Dubuque*
563-583-9261
dougnursery@aol.com

Walker's Green Space
2699 53rd Street
Vinton, IA 52349 *Benton*
319-474-2324

Wapsi Pines Nursery Landscape
6827 Wheeler Road
Dunkerton, IA 50626 *Black Hawk*

Windmill Landscape & Garden
520 Franklin Street
Center Point, IA 52213 *Linn*
319-849-2245

Windy Pines Greenhouse
276 Dorchester Drive
Dorchester, IA 52140 *Allamakee*

Blackmore Gardens
1007 4th Street SW
Mason City, IA 50401 *Cerro Gordo*
641-423-5104

Your Day Trip Planner for *Northeast Iowa*

I can't think of any gardener who wouldn't want to steal away at least one day in spring with a band of cohorts to take in sites of horticultural interest. But where to go can be a most vexing question with so many gardens and so little time. That's why I've composed the following day trip planner to assist you in your preparations for a day afield enjoying the bounty of Iowa's garden attractions. Though you're certainly free to put your own together, I thought you might enjoy this trip that I took once.

Best time of year: Summer
Estimated round-trip mileage: 10 miles
Number of places: 3

Spend an entire day in Dubuque! Northeast Iowa is rich in horticultural attraction but the city of Dubuque has a corner on the market when it comes to diversity and quality in such a small area. On many occasions, I've enjoyed visiting the **Dubuque Arboretum and Botanical Gardens**, located in the hills on the city's north side. In this, the only entirely volunteer-operated public garden in the United States, the exceptional collection of plants and ideas ranks it one of the best public gardens in the Midwest. With large collections of roses and dwarf conifers and a really large collection of hostas (rumored to be the largest assemblage open to public in the country), an entire day could easily be spent traipsing about the trails, looking at plants, taking in the serenity of well-groomed public park, and enjoying the company of a tireless troupe of volunteers.

Northeast Iowa

NE

But now with all these new ideas, it only seems fitting to hurry off to a nursery or garden center to find a few green goodies to bring home (and make someone else plant). You've got two great choices both within a mile of the Arboretum. If hostas are your thing, you'll want to look up **Jim's Hostas**. Jim and his wife have easily amassed one of the largest private collections of hostas that you've likely ever seen (that anyone's maybe ever seen!). In their yard, 3,700 cultivars will leave your head spinning in much the same feeling as you had after wild merry-go-round ride as a kid. The best thing though about Jim's Hostas, aside from the hostas, is the website you can send your friends to (the ones who didn't get to come).

A couple local eateries worth trying out, assuming you're tired of plant shopping and looking for a quick bite, are Hudson's Classic Grill and Mongolian Grill. Both aren't far from the hub of garden locations you'll tour. Complete with 50s-style jukeboxes and an old Hudson automobile in the front window, Hudson's Classic Grill [(563) 588-1024] is a throwback to a diner of another era. They are known for very friendly service and tasty fare too. If you're looking for something with more of an ethnic appeal, try to Mongolian Grill [(563) 582-1199] across from the Target store off Highway 20. Watch talented chefs stir-fry your lunch for you after you've selected from a buffet assortment of ingredients including seafood, fresh vegetables, and a palette of zippy sauces. Rest assured you'll find no gluey-MSG laden food here.

After sheer hosta ecstasy and a little lunch, it might be advisable to make your way over to **Steve's Ace Home and Garden Center**. This is quite possibly the best garden center at a hardware store I've ever seen. Normally I avoid them but these folks know what they're doing. And the selection, prices, and quality will cause you to start shoveling plants onto handy pull-carts they've so helpfully provided. You'll be amazed at the little goodies they carry; not only perennials for sun and shade but a pretty upscale selection of veggies and fruits too. If garden art or quirky flare for the yard is your thing, you'll be right at home.

Best time of year: Summer
Estimated round-trip mileage: 105 miles
Number of places: 3

Another summer trip tour of gardens worth taking in northeast Iowa starts at the weekend-project gone wild of Keith and Kelli Kovarik. **K& K Gardens**, located in Hawkeye, is a sprawling oasis of gardens, meandering paths, sheds, and lots of plants for sale. Keith and Kelli, who both work full-time jobs away from the project that has consumed both their and a neighbor's lot, are passionate gardeners who share your desire to create a peaceful oasis full of color, personality, and life. I think you'll agree after visiting that this creation is something you just have to see.

Another must-see in this neck of the woods is the famed **Willowglen Nursery**, which no doubt gets its notoriety from owners Lee and Lindsay Lee's frequent appearances on the PBS show The Perennial Gardener with Karen Strohbeen. Both talented horticulturists and artisans, Lee and Lindsay have a unique passion for marrying plant combinations that yield a natural, balanced, and aesthetically elegant look. You'll find new, unusual, and quintessential perennials at this rural

Decorah nursery set amongst the hills and on a road that will leave you wondering if you're there yet. Have no fear, the end reward is well worth every bend in the road.

Passion seems to be the theme here. While headed back to Decorah for a late lunch, you'll inevitably encounter blue signs pointing you east towards Heritage Farm home of the **Seed Savers Exchange**. Diane Ott Whealy and her team have grown this non-profit organization from a kitchen table idea to an internationally venerable marketplace for the rare and bizarre in vegetables, fruits, and flowers. Stop by the farm to enjoy the Lillian Goldman Visitors Center and surrounding display gardens. Enjoy in-season products like garlic, potatoes, and plant starts and all-season inventory like garden furniture, books, and tools. Since 1975 Seed Savers Exchange members have traded over one million samples of seeds.

Lunch options in Decorah are numerous. The town is full of eclectic shops and historical venues so you could easily spend the rest of the afternoon exploring. Which is just as well since one of my favorite places to eat is only open after 4:00 PM. If you're looking for someplace classy, yet reasonably priced, I'd suggest stopping by the in-house restaurant of the Hotel Winneshiek called Albert's. Known for their delicious barbeque and diverse wine selection, you can sit in the comfort of Albert's street-side dining room [(563) 382-4164], sipping wine, and licking BBQ sauce off your fingers while pondering over the day's finds.

Northeast Iowa

NE

Southwest Iowa

Growing up here has instilled in me a loving appreciation for the merry hills of the south coast of the Hawkeye state. Their pleasantries give the land a character of its own, dotted on ridges by barns, grain bins, and white clapboard farmhouses that overlook fingerling streams and creeks.

My love for gardening here is deep. Regional microclimates lie between bubbling mounds of old glacial loam from Glenwood to Mount Ayr. This soil is a gift in this part of the state. Verging on USDA Zone 6 is certainly not uncommon and many gardens in this part of the state feature a unique assortment of favorite "can't haves" or at least things you aren't *supposed* to have.

Nothing about southwest Iowa is particularly unusual but nothing is particularly ordinary either. The gardeners here are my neighbors and friends. Familiar faces of my childhood. Call it home boy bias, but I love these southern hills, and I hope you will too.

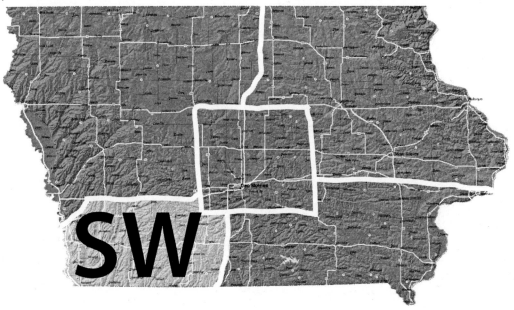

Canoyer Country Greenhouse
Amy Wyman
48597 Highway 92
Griswold, IA 51535 *Mills*
712-778-2200

When are they there? Seasonally. Mid-April to mid-June. Call for days open.
What are their hours? Call for hours.

Get to know them:
Canoyer's has two locations, one in Griswold and another in Papillion, Nebraska. The business started as the hobby of Craig and Kathy Canoyer with only 200 square feet under cover. Today they have several thousand square feet under cover and produce nearly all of their products themselves. It's the spirit of family in this operation that makes a trip to either location enjoyable and memorable. Canoyer's carries Proven Winners® products, perennials, annuals, trees, and shrubs. Their gift shop features a choice selection of statuary, pottery, and other gift items. Christmastime brings poinsettias and holiday gifts to the shelves.

Specialties:
Canoyer's strives to provide the highest quality products and reasonable prices. Personal attention to each customer is also a hallmark of their 20 plus years of success.

What about favorite plant?
Craig and Kathy's daughter Amy says her favorite plant is euphorbia Diamond Frost®. "You can use it for weddings with tropicals and in any containers." She adds "it's heat-tolerant and durable!"

David's Home & Garden Center
David Williams
315 Poplar Street
Atlantic, IA 50022 *Cass*
712-243-5682
davids@metc.net

When are they there? Year-round. April 15 to June 30 and November and December. Monday-Friday, Saturday, Sunday.

What are their hours? 9:00 AM to 6:00 PM, 9:00 AM to 5:00 PM, 12:00 PM to 5:00 PM

Get to know them:
David is a Master Gardener and started sharing his love and knowledge of plants with the Atlantic community in 2002 when he purchased a well-known garden center. "Most of our family of employees here are gardeners so we all have knowledge and love of plants, be it trees, shrubs, petunias, or hostas!" David says. This high-quality garden shop offers gardeners in the Atlantic area a one-stop shop and is well worth the visit.

Specialties:
David's is perhaps best known for a large selection of perennials and annuals, but an amazing line of containers, home decor, bird baths, trellises, and Christmas decorations abounds. From terra cotta to artificial trees, David's beautiful selection of gifts won't make it hard to find that perfect something for the gardener in the family.

What about favorite plant?
David's favorite plants are hostas. "They are so versatile," says David. "I have varieties that do well in the sun and those that thrive in the shade." He marvels at their many sizes, shapes, and forms too. "Hostas are the friendship plant. They're easy to grow and share!"

Southwest Iowa

SW

Lauritzen Gardens
100 Bancroft Street
Omaha, NE 68104
402-346-4002
d.myer@omahabotanicalgardens.org
www.lauritzengardens.org

Exit Hy 300

Do they charge admission? Yes.

When are they there? Year-round. Daily except Thanksgiving, Christmas, and New Year's Day.

What are their hours?
9:00 AM to 5:00 PM

Get to know them:
Though not officially an Iowa garden, this gem can't be missed when traveling around the southwest part of the state. Lauritzen Gardens, Omaha's Botanical Center, is an urban oasis on a 100-acre site. With walking paths, tram tours from May through October, a cafe open daily, a gift shop, festivals, and special events, the garden is the perfect outing for couples, families, and individuals looking for respite.

Specialties:
This living museum of plants features many different theme gardens including a rose garden, herb garden, Victorian garden, and a shade garden.

96

Southwest Iowa

SW

Southwest Iowa

SW

Southwest Iowa

Rainbow Iris Farm
Kenny, Krystal, Kelly & Kody Norris
3149 Kentucky Ave.
Bedford, IA 50833 *Taylor*
712-523-2807
irisfarm@frontiernet.net
www.rainbowfarms.net

SW

When are they there? Monday-Saturday, Sunday
What are their hours? 9:00 AM to 6:00 PM, 1:30 to 5:30 PM

Get to know them:
Founded in 1997 by the Cliff Snyder family of Bartlett, Texas, Rainbow Iris Farm was moved to Iowa in 2002 by the Norris family. The family-owned and -operated nursery was spearheaded by son Kelly and his passionate interest in irises and ornamental plants. Located south of Bedford, the nursery is located on seven acres of the family's farm. The Norrises offer nearly 1,500 cultivars of bearded irises in all colors of the rainbow. Bloomfest!, the farm's celebration of irises in bloom, is held annually at the end of May. Orders can be placed through their catalog, website, or on-site during open hours.

Specialties:
As the only certified iris nursery in the state, Rainbow Iris Farm is Iowa's and the Midwest's source for bearded irises.

What about favorite plant?
I won't be pressed to choose a favorite plant, favorite cultivar, or any other question that would journalistically indicate a preference to one thing or another (at least on the record.)

Southwest Iowa

SW

Rainbow Iris Farm

Southwest Iowa

SW

101

Southwest Iowa

SW

Wild by Nature
Doug & Cindy Sleep
1502 Madison Street
Bedford, IA 50833 *Taylor*
712-542-0105
sunnee96@yahoo.com

When are they there? Seasonally. Monday through Sunday.
What are their hours? 10:00 AM to 6:00 PM.

Get to know them:
A part-time business for a park ranger and a city employee, this small nursery has increased in size and scope since it opened. Focused on providing the area with well-grown and reasonably priced material, this is a great place to pick up just the right thing for that container or backyard bed you've been working on.

Specialties:
Doug and Cindy carry a well-grown selection of native grasses, hanging baskets, geraniums, and a yard full of mums each fall. Statuary, fountains, bird baths, unique containers, and nursery stock is also available.

Southwest Iowa

SW

Other Places of Interest in the SW Iowa Region

Bonnie Boswell
1307 State Highway 148
Corning, IA 50841 *Adams*
641-322-3516

Color My World
The Hodge Family *Day Lilies*
1363 320th Street
Bedford, IA 50833 *Taylor*

Country Blooms
Wanda Johnson
1875 Fontanelle Road
Fontanelle, IA 50846 *Adair*
641-745-3025
cblooms@mddc.com

Country Meadow Greenhouse
Bonnie Randles
1928 County Hwy. J43
Mount Ayr, IA 50854 *Ringgold*
641-464-2705

Henkeville Farm & Garden
Bob & Judy Henke
2235 "V" Avenue
Clarinda, IA 51632 *Page*
712-542-5302

Lehman's Greenhouse, LLC
Richard Lehman
21965 Barrus Rd.
Glenwood, IA 51534 *Mills*
712-527-5825
lehmansnursery@aol.com

Mother Earth Greenhouse
Joan R. Houser
46928 Pioneer Trail
Henderson, IA 51541 *Mills*
712-267-2736

Muddika/Hazel's Place
Marie Stephens
1834 County Highway J43
Mount Ayr, IA 50854 *Ringgold*
641-234-0018
muddika@iowatelecom.net
www.muddika.com

Oakcrest Gardens
Phyllis Randall
22871 Kane Ave.
Glenwood, IA 51534 *Mills*
712-527-4974

Your Day Trip Planner for *Southwest Iowa*

I can't think of any gardener who wouldn't want to steal away at least one day in spring with a band of co-horts to take in sites of horticultural interest. But where to go can be a most vexing question with so many gardens and so little time. That's why I've composed the following day trip planner to assist you in your preparations for a day afield enjoying the bounty of Iowa's garden attractions. Though you're certainly free to put your own together, I thought you might enjoy this trip that I took once.

Best time of year: Spring
Estimated round-trip mileage: 80 miles
Number of places: 3

I really don't mean to be egotistical here, but a spring day-trip in southwest Iowa would be remiss if you didn't stop at, and I didn't invite you to, my family's nursery, **Rainbow Iris Farm**. With seven acres of irises to enjoy and peruse, our passionate project has drawn thousands of visitors from the four-state area since the spring of 2003. If you're looking for a daylong extravaganza in and of itself, you should look up Bedford on the third Saturday in May. It's on this day that *Bedford in Bloom!*, Bedford's signature economic event, kicks off our three-week bloom season. The one-day event, which nearly doubles the size of our rural community, features a multitude of events for the family including gardening lectures, a BBQ competition, live entertainment, and a shuttle service to our farm.

While you're in the area, you could stray across the border (nobody will tell) to Maryville, Missouri to see seven acres of peonies at **Hollingsworth Peony Nursery.** Maintained by the ever vibrant Don and Lavon Hollingsworth and their manager Lucas Hudson, this operation will change your view of peonies. Their breeding work has garnered several American Peony Society Gold Medals. Notable introductions include the fuchsia bombshell 'Command Performance' and one of many golden wonders 'Garden Treasure'.

If you end up in Maryville for lunch and you're wise, you'll take in A&G Restaurant, Bar, & Grill [(660) 582-4421], hailed as Maryville's finest restaurant. With a well-rounded and diverse menu, you'll be able to reflect on the new peonies and irises you've just bought while enjoying an Italian or Greek entrée.

After taking in two specialty nurseries, it's always nice to return to something a little more mainstream. **Henkeville Farm & Garden** located east of Clarinda, Iowa (just a short 30-minute drive up Highway 71) features a well-grown assortment of annuals and perennials that owner Judy Henke is always trying to "keep different." And don't miss their fine-looking containers. Since you'll have only purchased and reserved product at the last two stops, you'll have the whole back end of the car to fill at your last stop. Why not get mom or the woman in your life one of those containers? Reward yourself with one too!

Southeast Iowa

Warm and friendly to a host of plants that would otherwise struggle in gardens farther north, southeast Iowa seems like Iowa's vacation spot particularly in early spring when fitful winter weather won't let go in Mason City or Fort Dodge.

Dusty roads, river vistas, and gradually more trees are common sights from the byways of this quadrant. Large tracts of old growth forests, remnants from an early era in our state's natural history, contain a profound gallery of wildflowers each spring. If you're botanically inclined, you might consider poking around Shimek and Stephens State Forests before heading off to a local nursery to seek out these fine natives for your own garden. Taking inspiration from native lands is one of my favorite things to do, especially when gifted with vantages so beautiful.

If you'd like to catch a head-start on spring, or just want to escape the waning days of winter for a short day, a number of off-the-path specialty houses are guaranteed to fill your car with the latest they have to offer.

SE

Denny's Greenhouses Ltd.
Denny & Donna Burk
1746 346th Ave.
Wever, IA 52658 *Lee*
319-372-1020
dennysgh@msn.com

When are they there? Year-round. Open daily except Christmas and Thanksgiving. Monday-Thursday, Friday-Saturday, Sunday.
What are their hours? 8:00 AM to 6:00 PM, 8:00 AM to 4:00 PM, 10:00 AM to 4:00 PM

Get to know them:
Denny's Greenhouses began in 1984 after the family had raised vegetables under the moniker Denny's Vegetables since 1973. The business is located at the family farm, a century farm no less, and wholesales account for 85 percent of their business. Retail customers are welcome though to browse through all 54 greenhouses which amounts to 120,000 square feet of production space.

Specialties:
Denny's is known for a large variety of annuals and perennials but especially their ornamental grass and vegetative annual selection. Larger pots of hardy hibiscus, grasses, garden mums, and asters are available in late summer and fall too.

What about favorite plant?
The Gerbera daisy is Denny's favorite plant. He appreciates their wide range of colors and large, beautiful daisy-like flowers and calls them winners for any garden.

Southeast Iowa

Forever Green, Inc.
Lucy & Mike Hershberger
125 Forevergreen Road
Coralville, IA 52241 *Johnson*
319-626-6770
forevergreen@southslope.net
www.forevergreengrows.com

SE

When are they there? Year-round. Daily.
What are their hours? Call for open hours.

Get to know them:
Forever Green is a 2-acre garden center known for its high-quality staff. "They are knowledgeable and enjoy helping everyone from beginners to avid gardeners," says owner Lucy Hershberger. An added bonus, recently opened, are on-site display gardens. A butterfly house featuring native butterfly species is also present and surely a favorite with children. Committed to education, Forever Green offers seminars throughout the season on a variety of landscaping and gardening topics.

Specialties:
Gardeners will find a large selection of trees, shrubs, annuals, perennials, gardening gifts, and landscaping supplies at Forever Green." We try to offer a good selection of the newest varieties and old favorites," says Lucy. They also offer professional landscaping design and installation services.

What about favorite plant?
" 'Carol Mackie' Daphne. Wait. No, a viburnum or maybe 'Twilight' coneflower. Do I really have to choose a favorite?" Lucy asks. Like many gardeners her favorite changes all the time. " 'Twilight' just caught my eye."

Southeast Iowa

SE

Hobbs Hilltop Gardens
Gerald Hobbs
2597 Highway 2
Fort Madison, IA 52627 *Lee*
319-372-4178
hobbshilltopgardens@msn.com

When are they there? Seasonally. Daily.
What are their hours? 9:00 AM to 7:00 PM

Get to know them:
"Come see us!" invites owner Gerald Hobbs of his Hilltop Gardens, the home of his daylily breeding program. Peak daylily bloom season runs from the first week in July into late August and visitors are welcome to peruse the seedling patch in search of new and exciting daylilies. This garden is a certified American Hemerocallis Society Display Garden.

Specialties:
With over 500 varieties of daylilies and 300 daylily seedlings of his own breeding, Hobbs Hilltop Gardens is the place in southeast Iowa to catch up on all that is happening with these summer-blooming perennial favorites. Also available are 50 varieties of hosta, 20 varieties of ornamental grasses, and various perennials.

SE

SE

Iowa City Landscaping
520 Hwy. 1 West
Iowa City, IA 52246 *Johnson*
319-337-8351
connect@iowacitylandscaping.net
www.iowacitylandscaping.net

When are they there? Year-round. Monday-Friday, Saturday, Sunday.
What are their hours? 8:00 AM to 6:00 PM, 9:00 AM to 5:00 PM, 10:00 AM to 5:00 PM

Get to know them:
Founded by brothers Paul and Dennis Dykstra and sister-in-law Linda Dysktra in 1982, this full-service landscaping business and garden center has grown into one of the largest in eastern Iowa. The nursery expanded into an old county maintenance facility in 1988 and carries an extensive selection of high-quality plants. A helpful, friendly staff is able to assist you with questions you might have.

Specialties:
Iowa City Landscaping is known for its large selection of plant material including different, unique conifers, shrub roses, broadleaf evergreens, grasses, perennials, and an upscale garden gift shop. Though classy, pricing is quite reasonable.

What about favorite plant?
Manager Chuck Porto jokes that his favorite plant is any one that people will buy.

Leichty Farm Greenhouse
Melanie Leichty
3393 330th Street
Wellman, IA 52356 *Washington*
319-646-5286

When are they there? Seasonally. Monday-Saturday.
What are their hours? 8:00 AM to 6:00 PM

Get to know them:
Leichty Farm Greenhouse is a very small, family-operated business. "Our greenhouse is 20 x 50 square feet and is located just behind our house," says owner Melanie.

Specialties:
They carry annuals, bedding plants, vegetable starts, hanging baskets, and the ever-popular Wave® petunias.

What about favorite plant?
Salvia 'Victoria Blue'. "It's so easy to care for and the color is beautiful." Melanie also notes it's striking appearance is against other plants.

Little Red Barn Greenhouses
Roxanne Nagel
20770 Utica Ridge Road
Davenport, IA 52804 *Scott*
563-505-7032
nagel@dwx.com

When are they there? Seasonally. Daily from April 15-June 15.
What are their hours? 8:00 AM to 6:00 PM

Specialties:
You'll find bedding plants, mixed containers, hanging baskets, cut flowers, pumpkins, mums, and vegetables at Little Red Barn Greenhouses. Look for them at the Davenport Farmers' Market as well.

What about favorite plant?
Roxanne can't be pressed to pick just one favorite so she says "all of them!"

Muscatine Arboretum
Muscatine, IA 52761 *Muscatine*
www.neighborhoodlink.com/org/muscaarboretum

Do they charge admission? No

When are they there? Year-round. Daily.
What are their hours? Sunrise to sunset.

Get to know them:
The Muscatine Arboretum was established in 1995. While the arboretum has no physical address, this civic project is well-worth finding in Muscatine (it's not far off of Hwy 61). The arboretum is located on county-owned property adjacent to the Environmental Discovery Center. Access is through the Discovery Center or from Houser Street via Harmony Lane. The Arboretum is presently striving to collect all nursery and landscape plants from the FFA identification list that will grow in Iowa. Their desire is to support the local FFA chapters' recent successful efforts at state and national competitions.

Specialties:
This public garden features a permanent collection of over 800 trees and shrubs for education, research, beautification, and conservation initiatives. Native prairie plants and wildflowers are also held in collection.

What about favorite plant?
A favorite plant among members of the arboretum's board is *Chamaecyparis nootkatensis*, the Alaskan cedar.

Southeast Iowa

SE

Ogle's Greenhouse & Garden Center
Mike Ogle
1717 South B. Street
Albia, IA 52531 *Monroe*
641-932-3444
oglemike@hotmail.com

When are they there? Seasonally. Monday-Saturday, Sunday.
What are their hours? 9:00 AM to 6:00 PM, 12:00 PM to 4:00 PM

Get to know them:
Operating from a new facility as of 2008, Ogle's started in 1978 as a flower shop. In 1994 a greenhouse was added and all growing operations are maintained on site. If you buy a plant at Ogle's, they've grown it.

Specialties:
"We pride ourselves in knowledgeable customer service and a real experience of exploring the greenhouse grounds." Ogle's offers perennials, heirloom tomatoes, vegetable plants, shrubs, and hundreds of ornamental trees.

What about favorite plant?
Gerbera daisy. "Great summer bloomer, classy, and does great inside throughout the winter," are all reasons Mike cites in justification of his choice.

Ostrander Flowers & Greenhouse
1243 25th Avenue
Eldon, IA 52554 *Wapello*
541-652-3288
ostranderflowers@hotmail.com

When are they there? Year-round. Monday-Saturday, Sunday.
What are there hours? 8:00 AM to 6:00 PM, 10:00 AM to 3:00 PM

Get to know them:
Now in its second generation, the business began in 1953 as a truck farm. Eventually the family expanded to 13 greenhouses and a full-service flower shop all still located on the original homestead along the scenic Des Moines River. Though flooded in 1993, they made floral deliveries by boat for three weeks.

Specialties:
You'll find a wide variety of geraniums, hanging baskets, a huge selection of perennials, and Proven Winners® at Ostrander's. The flower shop offers mixed wreaths and silk flower arrangements.

What about favorite plant?
"In this business you see so many plants that when you see something different the first time you love it until the next unique plant comes along," Kathy says. Otherwise she's awfully fond of lilacs for their spring flowering, fragrance, and ease of care.

Southeast Iowa

SE

Pleasant Valley Garden Center
Aleda Feuerbach
1301 South Gilbert Street
Iowa City, IA 52240 *Johnson*
319-337-3118
info@pleasantvalleyic.com
www.pleasantvalleyic.com

When are they there? Year-round. Monday-Saturday.
What are their hours? Call for open hours.

Get to know them:
Pleasant Valley Garden Center got its start in Holland in the early 1950s when Arie Kroeze and Toni Versteegh first met. After emigrating to the U.S. and settling in Iowa City, they began working at local greenhouses and doing landscape jobs. Their passion for horticulture led them to found Pleasant Valley Garden Center in the early 1960s. Arie and Tori's daughter Aleda continues to operate the business today with her family in the tradition with which it began. The company now owns a retail flower shoppe, golf course, and garden center.

Specialties:
You'll find a year-round supply of tropicals and houseplants at Pleasant Valley. But in season of course you'll find a variety of annuals, perennials, trees, and shrubs on their 2.5-acre nursery lot along with expert advice from a knowledgeable staff.

What about favorite plant?
Aleda's favorite plants are tricolor *Dracaena* and impatiens. She loves *Dracaena* because of its tropical appeal indoors and impatiens because they're an inexpensive source of color.

Red Fern Farm
Tom Wahl & Kathy Dice
13882 "I" Ave.
Wapello, IA 52653 *Louisa*
319-729-5905
redfernfarm@lisco.com
www.redfernfarm.com

When are they there? Year-round and by appointment.
What are their hours? Call for an appointment.

Get to know them:
Red Fern Farm is named after the course-lobed grape fern (*Botrychium dissectum*) that grows in the woods of Tom and Kathy's farm. It emerges in the fall, turns maroon-red after the first frost and lives all winter only to go dormant once spring returns. The family-owned nursery is a site for ongoing research of tree crops and forest farming systems. Their motto is aptly "a nursery of trees and ideas."

Specialties:
Red Fern Farm specializes in high-value crop-bearing trees and shrubs including chestnuts, hazel, persimmon, paw paw, and heartnut.

What about favorite plant?
Tom says chestnuts are his favorite plants. When asked why he says unabashedly that "they will save the world." "The culinary versatility of chestnuts coupled with sustainable techniques used to produce them amount to a more efficient system of crop production than most of the major grain commodities," says Tom.

SE

Schiller's Flowers & Foliage
Ernest & Cheryl Schiller
2065 Highway 2
Donnellson, IA 52625 *Lee*
319-835-5601
ernestschiller@hotmail.com
www.locateaflowershop.com/states/IA/Donnellson.asp

When are they there? Year-round. Daily.
What are their hours? Call for open hours.

Get to know them:
Ernest and Cheryl opened their business 35 years ago out of a love for unusual plants. Despite growth and change over the years, they still pride themselves for their customer service and unusual selection of perennials and shrubbery.

Specialties:
In addition to a full-service flower shop, the greenhouse and nursery offers unique shrubs, unusual perennials, and hardy grasses. Statuary, water fountains, ceramics, and bird baths are also for sale.

What about favorite plant?
Bromeliads are favorites of Ernest and Cheryl because of their long-lasting, interesting, and unique blooms, and they don't outgrow their containers!

Sunnyslope Greenhouse
Delmar & Marilyn Vos
1621 Highway 163
Leighton, IA 50143 *Mahaska*
641-626-3702
sunnyslope@iowatelecom.net

When are they there? Year-round. Monday-Friday, Saturday.
What are their hours? 8:00 AM to 7:00 PM, 8:00 AM to 5:00 PM

Get to know them:
Located right along Highway 163 and not far from Tassel Ridge Winery, Sunnyslope is a favorite spot in spring for local gardeners. If you live in southeast Iowa and haven't been, find a friend a go out for a road trip.

Specialties:
Sunnyslope carries an extensive line of geraniums including 65 cultivars of regals, exotics, and ivies abounding in all colors. A large variety of bedding plants, perennials, containers, and much more can be found. The unique country shop is the place to pick up a varied assortment of gardening supplies.

Southeast Iowa

SE

Tender Top Gardens
Sue Kershner
2902 Highway 406 Road
West Burlington, IA 52655 *Des Moines*
319-752-3305

When are they there? Seasonally. April-September. Tuesday-Saturday, Sunday.
What are their hours? 9:00 AM to 6:00 PM, 12:00 PM to 5:00 PM.

Get to know them:
In business since 1988, Tender Top Gardens is southeast Iowa's source for DIY water gardening supplies and plants. The Kershners' yard serves as the show room with daylilies, hostas, dwarf conifers, and many shrubs planted so that customers can see mature specimens. Four water gardens home to resident koi have been installed for enjoyment.

Specialties:
Tender Top Gardens carries a full line of DIY water garden supplies and assorted fish to stock your new water garden. If you're looking for water garden plants then you're in luck too. Over 100 varieties of water lilies, lotus, and bog plants are stocked. Garden art isn't missing from their inventory either.

What about favorite plant?
Sue's favorite plant is Dave (yes they gave their favorite plant a person's name). It's really a *Pinus contorta* 'Taylor's Sunburst', the golden-tipped shore pine. "When we planted it, it was only 3 feet tall but now is over 6 feet. It has the most amazing, chartreuse yellow needles in May and June", says Sue. It's planted near an entrance to their home so they can see it multiple times daily.

Southeast Iowa

The Landscaper & Nursery, Inc.
Gary Garles
2371 Kale Boulevard
Fairfield, IA 52556 *Jefferson*
641-472-7129
sunshine@lisco.com

SE

When are they there? Seasonally. Monday-Saturday.
What are their hours?
8:00 AM to 5:00 PM.

Specialties:
The Landscaper & Nursery specialize in hostas and prides themselves for having an Iowa-certified nurseryman on staff.

What about favorite plant?
Hosta nigrescens 'Elatior'. "It looks way too big and tropical for Iowa but that's what makes it cool. Blooms up to 6-7 feet tall!"

SE   **Vander Veer Botanical Park**
Susan Anderson
214 W. Central Park Ave.
Davenport, IA 52803 *Scott*
563-323-3298
sgo@ci.davenport.ia.us
www.cityofdavenportiowa.com

Do they charge admission? No

When are they there? Year-round. Tuesday-Saturday, Sunday.
What are their hours? 10:00 AM to 4:00 PM, 12:00 PM to 4:00 PM.

Get to know them:
Vander Veer Botanical Park was established in 1885 on 33 acres of parkland in Davenport. Home to a conservatory, hosta glade, rose garden and many other display areas, the park is famous for its 100-year tradition of floral and tropical plant shows. Continuous displays are presented year-round including a Winter Azalea Show, the Spring Floral Show, the Easter Lily Show, the Fall Chrysanthemum Show, and the Poinsettia & Lights display.

Specialties:
The park features beautiful collections of ornamental horticulture, including three nationally recognized gardens, teaching areas, and the Conservatory complex. Approximately 55,000 visitors visit each year.

Southeast Iowa

Washington Garden Decor & Greenhouses, Inc.
Nina & Mike Tadlock
1820 West Main Street
Washington, IA 52353 *Washington*
319-653-2471
washnursery@iowatelecom.net

SE

When are they there? Year-round. Call for open days.
What are their hours? Call for open hours.

Get to know them:
The store was built in 1994 and has five greenhouses that carry a full line of gardening necessities. All of the plants available for sale have been grown on-site and customers are always thrilled with the selection. Nina and Mike select all of the varieties themselves, choosing plants that will thrive in our Iowa climate.

Specialties:
"We feel confident in saying that we are best known for the quality, health, and variety of annuals and perennials of our garden center," says owner Nina. They also should pride themselves on customer service as you'll more than likely be greeted by Nina or Mike as they are there most of the time.

What about favorite plant?
Nina and Mike chose favorites based on light exposure. "For sun it would be sedum because it's tough, drought tolerant, and easy. For shade it would be heuchera. There are so many new colors to add bright spots to shady areas."

Southeast Iowa

Other Places of Interest in the SE Iowa Region

Aunt Rhodie's Design Studio
Todd Wiebenga
2012 E. 11th Street
Davenport, IA 52803 *Scott*
563-323-2840
aunt_rhodies@hotmail.com
www.auntrhodies.com

Carter Nursery
1515 West Mount Pleasant Street
West Burlington, IA 52655
Des Moines

Centerville Greenhouse
Rob Lind
5th & Van Buren
Centerville, IA 51501 *Appanoose*

Everdina's Greenhouse
Everdina Butler
9572 82nd St.
Ottumwa, IA 52501 *Wapello*
641-684-7949

Fiddlehead Gardens
Curtis Schoenthaler
P.O. Box 621
Iowa City, IA 52244 *Johnson*
319-321-6549

Frida's Hosta.com
Allen & Jayne Wiese
3324 Diehn Avenue
Davenport, IA 52802 *Scott*
563-326-4590
www.hosta.com

Garden Gate Greenhouse
1200 Columbus Street
Pella, IA 50219 *Marion*

Gruber's Glad Garden
1973 Wisconsin Avenue
Davenport, IA 52806 *Scott*
563-324-0168

Herrmann's Greenhouse
123 North Jefferson Street
Ottumwa, IA 52501 *Wapello*

HostasGalore
34 Gas Lantern Square
Muscatine, IA 52761 *Muscatine*
563-299-4113

Indian Prairie Greenhouse
Marilee Miller
14896 Rte. J40
Milton, IA 52570 *Van Buren*
641-656-4473
ipg66mmt@iowatelecom.net

Southeast Iowa

SE

Oakwood Nursery & Garden
Terri Jane Diers & Terry Merl Klein
P.O. Box 44, 1000 Oakwood Blvd.
Fairfield, IA 52556 *Jefferson*
641-472-6775

Outdoor Artistry Nursery & Landscape
305 East Lincolnway Street
Jefferson, IA 50129 *Greene*

Reeves Wildflower Nursery
28431 200th Street
Harper, IA 52231 *Keokuk*

Reha Greenhouses
1160 Highway 22
Wellman, IA 52356 *Washington*
319-646-2408

Ritter's Garden Center
Stephen Ritter
924 Broadway
West Burlington, IA 52655
Des Moines
319-752-3679
iaplntman@aol.com

Rose Hill Nursery
2282 Teller Road
Rose Hill, IA 52586 *Mahaska*

Stam Greenhouse
Brent & Phyllis Stam
2421 Hwy. 92
Oskaloosa, IA 52577 *Mahaska*
641-672-1437
eaestam@lisco.com

Suburban Garden Center
PO Box 1510
Davenport, IA 52809 *Scott*

Sunnyview Greenhouse
56665 Hazelwood Avenue SW
Kalona, IA 52247 *Washington*
319-656-2589

Temple Lane Hostas
DeEtta Montgomery
2 Temple Lane
Davenport, IA 52803 *Scott*
563-323-4385

Teske's Pet & Garden Center
2395 Spruce Hills Drive
Bettendorf, IA 52722 *Scott*

Southeast Iowa

SE

The Berry-Pine Place
Guerden and Carol Christensen
2466 Henry Ladyn Dr.
Montrose, IA 52639 *Lee*
319-463-5676

The Green Thumbers
Charles Rickey
5112 Grandview
Muscatine, IA 52761 *Muscatine*
563-263-4403

The Secret Garden
Kristen & Ryan Gourley
10182 Danville Rd.
Danville, IA 52623 *Des Moines*
319-392-8288
ryan@the-secret-garden.net
www.the-secret-garden.net

Thymely Solutions
104 N. Court St.
Fairfield, IA 52556 *Jefferson*
641-472-9815

Wallace's Garden Center &
Greenhouses
2605 Devils Glen Rd.
Bettendorf, IA 52722 *Scott*
563-332-4711

Walnut Hill Gardens
Barrett Stoll
999 310th Street
Atalissa, IA 52720 *Muscatine*
563-946-3471

Your Day Trip Planner for *Southeast Iowa*

I can't think of any gardener who wouldn't want to steal away at least one day in spring with a band of co-horts to take in sites of horticultural interest. But where to go can be a most vexing question with so many gardens and so little time. That's why I've composed the following day trip planner to assist you in your preparations for a day afield enjoying the bounty of Iowa's garden attractions. Though you're certainly free to put your own together, I thought you might enjoy this trip that I took once.

Best time of year: Summer
Estimated round-trip mileage: 112 miles
Number of places: 3

Iowa City is fortunate to have two high-quality nurseries right within its city limits. I'd first suggest stopping by **Iowa City Landscaping** on Highway 1. Hands-down, this is a fine garden center. Trees, shrubs, perennials, you name it and they've got it in stock. I've always been impressed with the selection within each of those groups too and with such good deals on most products it's not hard to walk away with several flats at a time. They also aren't a one-season shopping mart either. They're open through the entire growing season, especially convenient for as many times as I find myself in Iowa City during the summer months. I've probably got a whole bed somewhere that came from this high-quality retailer.

Farther north you'll find an Iowa City gardening tradition, **Pleasant Valley Garden Center**. Though they've got excellently grown trees, shrubs, and nursery stock from the best wholesale growers, I was most impressed with their indoor facility and array of tropicals and houseplants, heady praise coming from an apathetic cultivator of plants indoors. I'd imagine that many spring-sick locals wander in here in about February and peruse the tropicals in search of inspiration or green-leaved cheer. Either way this stop has year-round potential.

Iowa City and Coralville are great cities to eat in. But to keep the theme of fine, local cuisine and dining I'd recommend Atlas World Grill [(319) 341-7700]. Though a little pricier than your average lunch stop, for a day out on the town you deserve this. The menu is flattering, rich, and assorted. Appetizers, salads, and entrees will leave you relishing the days of summer and refreshed for the drive to Davenport.

Davenport itself has a variety of horticultural destinations of interest that you'll also want to check out. But I thought you might like to enjoy a fine public garden and you can do so at the 33-acre **Vander Veer Park**, located between Brady and Harrison Streets, just south of West Central Park Avenue. The conservatory is renowned for its floral displays, carrying on a 100-year tradition with events like the Easter Lily Show. But for a summer visit you'll most certainly appreciate the All-American Rose Selections test garden and an exotic vegetable garden.

Central Iowa

An integral chapter of my gardening life has taken place in Ames as I pursued my bachelor's degree in horticulture at Iowa State. Though populous and busy, Central Iowa is rich in horticultural opportunities with many of the state's largest retailers of green materials calling the area home. If you can't find it here, you're looking for something pretty rare or unusual.

Growing up hours away gives you a fresh take on what you find after your parents drop you off at college and wave goodbye. You value what you have known and relish what you haven't. Central Iowa is home to the majority of Iowa's public gardens, all of which offer you a palette of ideas for crafting your own dream garden. Day-trip possibilities are endless as you'll see at the end of the section too.

With two major interstate highways transecting the region, traveling is quick, efficient (save the always present road construction), and a car of day-trippers can handedly cover the gamut in the better part of a day. But the number of back roads and country byways available certainly merit travel, especially if you'd rather escape the bustle.

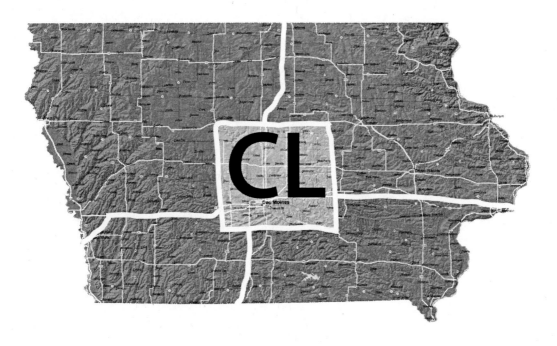

Central Iowa

CL

Brenton Arboretum
Kay Meyer
25141 260th Street
Dallas Center, IA 50063 *Dallas*
515-992-4211
info@thebrentonarboretum.org
www.thebrentonarboretum.org

Do they charge admission? No

When are they there? Year-round. Tuesday-Sunday
What are their hours? 9:00 AM to sunset

Get to know them:
The Brenton Arboretum is a living museum of trees and shrubs set amongst native prairie and a lake. Visitors can enjoy strolls on a variety of trails where they will likely see a number of butterflies, birds, and other wildlife. But if you'd rather enjoy the arboretum from your car, a two-mile auto trail through the park is available. Scenic and pastoral, this rural landscape has been owned by the Brenton family since 1853. The arboretum was founded by Sue and Buz Brenton because of their love of trees and their desire to preserve the nature world. The arboretum's growing collections of woody ornamentals are frequently used by researchers and arborists from around the Midwest.

Specialties:
This living museum of trees and shrubs will only continue to improve in quality and quantity with age. Trails, bridges, streams, and Lake Homestead welcome visitors from all over to this little piece of Iowa's native landscape.

CypHaven
Carson Whitlow
22957 280th Street
Adel, IA 50003 *Dallas*
515-993-4841
Slipperguy@aol.com
www.c-we.com/cyp.haven

When are they there? Not generally open to the public. Mail-order.

Get to know them:
CypHaven is the breeding facility and mail-order nursery of world-renowned orchid expert Carson Whitlow. Carson works with lady's slipper orchids (*Cypripedium*) in addition to the genera *Calopogon* and *Pogonia*. He offers his selections for sale through his website.

Specialties:
Cypripediums and other native orchids are Carson's specialty.

Central Iowa

CL

Des Moines Feed & Garden Shoppe
Ralph Holt
2019 Hubbell Avenue
Des Moines, IA 50317 *Polk*
515-262-0154

When are they there? Year-round. Monday-Friday.
What are their hours? 8:00 AM to 6:00 PM

Specialties:
At this central Iowa garden shop you'll find new and special perennials, annuals, roses, woody ornamentals, conifers, and even fruit trees. Statuary, fountains, planters, gardening supplies, and much more can be found at this conveniently stocked store.

Evergreen Gardens
Pam Maurer
6036 George Washington Carver
Ames, IA 50010 *Story*
515-232-7633
pam@evergreen-gardens.com
www.evergreen-gardens.com

When are they there? Seasonally and by appointment. Tuesday-Friday.
What are their hours? 1:00 PM to 6:00 PM

Get to know them:
Pam Maurer's business began in 2007 with the help of dwarf conifer connoisseur Gary Whittenbaugh. Pam's love for dwarf and unusual conifers surrounds her home for customers to see and enjoy. This new nursery will surely become a gem for dwarf conifer collectors and trough gardeners. If you're near Ames you should check up on Pam and find a new evergreen to take home.

Specialties:
Dwarf conifers and alpines for rock gardens and troughs are Pam's sole specialties. Visit her website for a complete plant list.

What about favorite plant?
Dwarf conifer collectors usually can't be forced to pick, and for good reason!

Central Iowa

CL

Flying Frog Farms LLC
Marsha & Bruno Ansevics
5148 155th Avenue
Indianola, IA 50125 *Warren*
515-961-3585
flyingfrogfarm@aol.com
www.flyingfrogfarms.com

When are they there? Seasonally. Tuesday-Sunday.
What are their hours?
9:00 AM to 5:00 PM

Get to know them:
Flying Frog Farm is a 3-acre hosta haven located just south of Des Moines. Display beds and shade houses are open for visitors to walk through and enjoy. A quaint gift shop features an assortment of eclectic "gardener's-only" gifts.

Specialties:
Marsha and Bruno grow 800 different hosta cultivars and a host of companion plants for the shade garden.

What about favorite plant?
Obviously hostas, so I pressed Marsha for her favorite cultivar. She says 'Guardian Angel' is her favorite because of its many shades of green and grey that don't seem possible.

Goode Greenhouses, Inc.
James P. Goode
1050 NE 50th Ave.
Des Moines, IA 50313 *Polk*
515-262-6504
goodegreenhouse@mchsi.com
www.goodes.com

When are they there? Year-round. Monday-Saturday, Sunday.
What are their hours? 8:00 AM to 5:00 PM, 12:00 PM to 4:00 PM.

Get to know them:
Goode Greenhouses is a family operated business that began in 1905. They've grown to become Iowa's largest retail bedding plant grower with over 40,000 square feet of indoor shopping space. A friendly atmosphere coupled with an excellent selection of bedding plants make a stop at Goode's well worth the visit. You'll easily spend hours just roaming around through all their greenhouses.

Specialties:
Geraniums, bedding plants, and perennials are their spring specialties but also look for poinsettias and Easter lilies in season. Fountains, glazed pottery, and other garden decor is available in the garden center year-round.

What about favorite plant?
Geraniums are a favorite at Goode's. And when you produce thousands and thousands of them, why not?

Central Iowa

CL

Groth Gardens
Debra A. Groth
2451 Cumming Road
Winterset, IA 50273 *Madison*
515-462-4445
demagroth@l2speed.net
www.grothsgardens.com

When are they there? Seasonally. April 15-October 31. Monday-Saturday, Sunday.
What are their hours? 9:00 AM to 6:00 PM, 12:00 PM to 4:00 PM.

Get to know them:
Deb and her husband Marvin, and their two kids began selling sweet corn as a family business in 1990 in the back of an old pickup truck. Sweet corn, though, has given way to five greenhouses (the first in 1997) and a thriving business known for its 6,000 plant mum crop each fall and high-quality container gardens in spring. Farmers as well as nursery owners, the Groths transform their family farm into a garden center each spring with the arrival of customers from as far away as 200 miles. "It has been a rewarding experience to establish a business from the ground up," says Deb.

Specialties:
Unusual and hard-to-find perennials, shrub roses, specialty annuals, and Deb's designer mixed hanging baskets and containers are a few of this horticultural family's specialties. Don't forget their outstanding mum crops in the fall either.

What about favorite plant?
Deb's favorite plant is 'Limelight' hydrangea. "Easy care, long season of bloom, and you can even dry the flower heads," she says.

Central Iowa

Harvey's Floral Co.
Don & Mary Harvey
611 Nile Kinnick Drive South
Adel, IA 50003 *Dallas*
515-993-3916
MryHarvey@aol.com
www.harveyfloral.com

CL

When are they there? Year-round. Daily.

What are their hours? Call for open hours.

Get to know them:
Mary, and her late husband Don, have tended one of Central Iowa's best kept secrets for 40 years. Located just a few miles from where Don sold cut gladiolas with his father as a child, the one-acre complex contains about every plant imaginable. The vast selection will easily keep you enthralled for hours. The knowledgeable staff, including many Master Gardeners, is the cherry on top.

Specialties:
Anything that grows. From herbs, to houseplants, cacti, annuals, perennials, and scented geraniums, you'll have a hard time not finding what you're looking for at Harvey's.

141

CL Heirloom Gardens, Ltd.
Jeffrey C. Brennan
29154 360th Street
Van Meter, IA 50261 *Dallas*
515-996-2466
JBren92752@aol.com
www.heirloom-gardens.com

When are they there? Seasonally. Monday-Saturday, Sunday.
What are their hours? 9:00 AM to 5:00 PM, 12:00 PM to 4:00 PM

Get to know them:
Heirloom Gardens is a specialty grower of perennials that began as the project of Sharon Barak in 1989. Heirloom Gardens quickly grew to offer 500 different varieties of perennials, annuals, and herbs on 8,000 square feet of growing space. Jeff Brennan took over the business in 2003 carrying on the tradition of offering high-quality products and unusual garden art. The business family is also committed to educating the public through its many how-to classes and seminars throughout the growing season. A local artisan exhibit is another special event that has grown to be quite popular.

Specialties:
Heirloom Gardens carries extensive offerings of perennials, annuals, flowering shrubs, roses, heirloom tomatoes and vegetables, and eclectic outdoor accessories.

What about favorite plant?
Jeff is fond of all the new coneflowers on the market. 'Harvest Moon', 'Pink Double Delight', and 'Coconut Lime' are but a few of his favorite cultivars.

Central Iowa

Hill Top Greenhouses, Ltd.
Ronald F. Bittle
991 222nd Drive
Ogden, IA 50212 *Boone*
515-275-2229

CL

When are they there? Year-round. Monday-Saturday, Sunday.
What are their hours? 9:00 AM to 5:00 PM, 12:00 PM to 5:00 PM

Get to know them:
Hill Top Greenhouses is a retail and wholesale operation with 100,000 square feet of growing space. They are also one of the few growers in the state who maintain fresh annuals through August, making them the place to pick up supplies for fall containers.

Specialties:
Mixed patio containers, fresh annuals all growing season, perennials, and mums and asters in fall are just some of the many items you'll come across at Hill Top. Easter lilies and poinsettias are also available in-season.

Central Iowa

CL

Holub Garden & Greenouses, Inc.
Mike Holub
22085 580th Avenue
Ames, IA 50010 *Story*
515-232-4769
mjhscuba@aol.com

When are they there? Year-round. Monday-Friday, Saturday, Sunday.
What are their hours? 9:00 AM to 6:00 PM, 9:00 AM to 5:00 PM, 12:00 PM to 5:00 PM

Get to know them:
Holub's is a family business with a long history of supplying high-quality products to central Iowa gardeners. The main range of greenhouses was built in 1974 to be a national distribution center for New Guinea impatiens whose development was pioneered at Iowa State by Dr. Jack Weigel.

Specialties:
Holub's offers the finest quality bedding plants, hanging baskets, perennials, houseplants and even poinsettias at Christmas.

What about favorite plant?
Owner Mike Holub jokes that his favorite plant is the one in the customer's cart. "Seriously it's the ming aralia because then we won't have to water it the day after it sells."

Central Iowa

CL

145

CL

Hosta Hideaway
Dan & Kathy Ripperger
511 East Salem Avenue
Indianola, IA 50125 *Warren*
515-961-8213
dkripp@mchsi.com
http://www.hostahideaway.net/

When are they there? Seasonally. Monday-Saturday, Sunday
What are their hours? 9:00 AM to 5:30 PM, 1:00 PM to 4:00 PM

Get to know them:
Dan and Kathy have recently relocated their retail sales to nearby Green Acres Garden Center due to losing shade trees from Dutch Elm disease. They are still publishing a pricelist.

Specialties:
Dan and Kathy carry over 600 cultivars of hostas and admire them for their versatility, low maintenance, and the incredible number of varieties on the market.

Howell Greenhouse & Floral
Fred Howell
3145 Howell Court
Cumming, IA 50061 *Madison*
515-981-0863
flowerfarmerfred@aol.com
www.howellfloral.com

When are they there? Year-round. Daily.
What are their hours? 10:00 AM to 5:00 PM

Get to know them:
A short drive from Des Moines will lead you to 15 acres of cut flowers grown for dried arrangements and crafts. The Howell family has been growing fragrant fields of flowers since 1985. A year full of activities is always in store at Howell's including spring plant sales from their greenhouse and fall sales to celebrate the harvest. Pumpkins, corn shocks, and mums are all available. Winter and Christmas are also special times because of the extensive array of holiday centerpieces, dried arrangements, and potpourri for sale during their Christmas Open House.

Specialties:
Howell's grows sweet annie, gomphrena, salvia, static, globe thistle, sunflowers, celosia, and many more annuals in their fields. Tour their barn and see the haymow full of cut flowers hanging to dry. It's really a sight and smell to behold.

CL

Iowa Arboretum
1875 Peach Avenue
Madrid, IA 50156 *Boone*
515-795-3216
info@iowaarboretum.org
www.iowaarboretum.org

Do they charge admission? Donations are appreciated.

When are they there? Year-round. Call for open days.

What are their hours? Sunrise to sunset.

Get to know them:
The Iowa Arboretum is a 378-acre facility tucked amongst the bucholic scenery of Boone County. The 40 acres under cultivation are known as a "Library of Living Plants" and feature an esteemed collection of dwarf conifers, native Iowa hardwoods, unusual deciduous trees, and several perennial beds with ornamental grasses. Several events are held throughout the year that are open to the public including a grass sale and guided tour of the *Miscanthus* collection each September.

Specialties:
The Arboretum has extensive collections of many woody ornamentals and herbaceous perennials.

Central Iowa

CL

149

Central Iowa

CL

Central Iowa

Isle of Green Garden Center
Lorna Finch
609 South 9th Street
Marshalltown, IA 50158 *Marshall*
641-752-1999
lorna@isleofgreen.com
www.isleofgreen.com

CL

When are they there? Seasonally. May-June.
What are their hours? Call for open hours.

Get to know them:
Family-owned Isle of Green Garden Center is a staple of the gardening community in the Marshalltown area. Their massive inventory and friendly, knowledgeable staff will help you select plants and even a design for your garden. A complete plant list is available on their website.

Specialties:
Isle of Green carries 550 varieties of annuals, 400 varieties of perennials, 100 varieties of vegetables including many herbs, shrubs, small fruits, and even houseplants. Garden furniture and garden accessories are also available in the gift shop.

Central Iowa

CL

Nature's Garden
Mark & Pat Johnson
1089 44th Street
Des Moines, IA 50311 *Polk*
515-277-3052

When are they there? Seasonally and by appointment. First full weekend in June. Saturday-Sunday.
What are their hours? 9:00 AM to 5:00 PM

Get to know them:
Mark and Pat Johnson started growing plants for sale in 1994. But they've grown from a humble, few hundred plants to selling 3,000 plants at their open house in early June. "I start the plants from seed, specializing in the old-fashioned and unusual," says Pat. The Johnsons' gardens also offer visitors the opportunity to see plants at work. The gardens are also available for private tour starting in mid-June by appointment.

Specialties:
Nature's Garden offers an array of unique perennials as well as a few annuals and herbs. Mark also makes country benches and Adirondack-style chairs.

What about favorite plant?
"All of them!" says Pat. "Those that I grow from seed are my babies." How could she choose then?

Pantheon Hosta Gardens
Joyce M. Flies
19477 "T" Ave.
Dallas Center, IA 50063 *Dallas*
515-992-3805
jmflies@aol.com

Do they charge admission? No

When are they there? By-appointment.
What are their hours? Call for an appointment.

Get to know them:
Pantheon Hosta Gardens began as a backyard project to control erosion in a hillside garden. The garden features many sitting areas near a dry steam and a real, babbling brook set amongst a sea of hostas, 3,500 plants to be exact. The garden has taken on a mythological theme, aptly so considering the name, with beds being named for gods and goddesses that pertain to nature.

Specialties:
Hostas, of course, as well as other shade perennials like ferns and pulmonarias.

What about favorite plant?
Of the 1,500 varieties Joyce Flies grows none can be called her favorite. "I can find something delightful in each and every one," she says. "I like hostas because of the wide range of foliage, color, size, texture, and shape. And the older the plant, the more beautiful it becomes."

Central Iowa

CL

Perennial Gardens by Linda Grieve, Inc.
Linda Grieve
1633 NW 84th Ave.
Ankeny, IA 50023 *Polk*
515-964-7702
lindagrieve@perennialgardens.biz
www.perennialgardens.biz

When are they there? By appointment. Monday-Saturday
What are their hours? Call for open hours.

Get to know them:
Linda Grieve is an active member of the Iowa horticulture industry. Her passion for perennials can be seen in the gardens she designs and the plants she offers at her nursery. The business began out of a need for high-quality landscaping services in the Des Moines area in 1996.

Specialties:
Landscape design services are their specialty but the nursery offers unusual perennials and the newest trees and shrubs. Education is also a priority and the staff at Perennial Gardens is knowledgeable and helpful.

Central Iowa

Piney Ridge Greenhouses, Inc.
Ron & Ann Borwick
6355 NW 51st Street
Johnston, IA 50131 *Polk*
515-276-9554

CL

When are they there? Seasonally. April 1-June 14. Daily.
What are their hours? Call for open hours.

Get to know them:
Piney Ridge Greenhouses has been growing in Johnston since 1975. They carry an extensive selection of hard-to-find plants at some of the best prices in central Iowa. They're also known for their experienced staff (many of whom are Master Gardeners) and their custom container design service.

Specialties:
You'll find a wide array of new and old varieties of annuals and perennials at Piney Ridge in addition to a "true hosta-lover's collection of hostas." You'll find great pottery and gifts along with some exceptional containers as well.

Central Iowa

CL

Reiman Gardens
1407 University Boulevard
Ames, IA 50011 *Story*
515-294-2710
reimangardens@iastate.edu
www.reimangardens.iastate.edu

Do they charge admission? Yes

When are they there? Year-round. Monday-Friday.
What are their hours? 9:00 AM to 4:30 PM.

Get to know them:
Reiman Gardens is one of Iowa's largest and most familiar public gardens situated on a 14-acre site on the south end of the Iowa State University campus. This award-winning facility features distinct outdoor gardens, an indoor conservatory, 2,500-square-foot indoor butterfly wing, butterfly emergence cases, a gift shop, and five supporting greenhouses. It was established by a generous gift from Roy and Bobbi Jo Reiman in 1994.

Specialties:
Reiman is where the roses are at. It's home to the largest Griffith Buck rose collection in the nation, an All-America

Rose Selections garden, and the first in the nation sustainable rose garden. You'll also find the display gardens changing yearly to reflect different themes the garden takes on. The Christina Reiman Butterfly Wing is also a popular stop year-round.

Central Iowa

CL

Reiman Gardens

Skycrest Gardens
Tom & Marilyn Kenney
243 Dave Circle
Ames, IA 50010 *Story*
515-233-1382
skycrest2@mchsi.com

When are they there? Seasonally. Friday, Saturday, Sunday.
What are their hours? 12:00 PM to 8:00 PM, 9:00 AM to 5:00 PM, 12:00 PM to 5:00 PM.

Get to know them:
Skycrest Gardens has been in business since 1993 at Tom and Marilyn's home. The 3/4-acre lot is jam-packed with display beds of perennials and five different water gardens. While only open in the spring, this garden is fine to behold in all four seasons and you'll definitely come away with ideas. Both are quite knowledgeable when it comes to water garden installation and have encouraged many to dig one in their own backyard.

Specialties:
Skycrest offers perennials, a large number of hostas, water garden plants and supplies for sale. A list of hosta cultivars for sale is available.

What about favorite plant?
Tom and Marilyn are evidently partial to hostas, mainly because the latter are so carefree and easy-going.

Central Iowa

CL

Central Iowa

CL

Ted Lare Design Build
Ted Lare
2701 Cumming Avenue
Cumming, IA 50061 *Warren*
515-981-1075
lareland@aol.com
www.tedsgardens.com

When are they there? Seasonally. Monday-Saturday.
What are their hours? 9:00 AM to 5:00 PM.

Get to know them:
Ted Lare Design Build has been a landscaping design and installation firm for 26 years. In 2008 they expanded by building a brand new facility on 88 acres of land that includes a brand new garden center, greenhouse, design offices, and a great outdoor showroom with patios, streams, ponds, walls, and gardens. "It's truly spectacular," says owner Ted Lare.

Specialties:
At Ted's Garden Center you'll find unique and hard-to-find plants like large size Japanese maples, topiaries, spirals, as well as an assortment of traditional landscape plants. Fountains, garden art, pots and planters, patio furniture, arbors, trellises, books and gift items are also available.

What about favorite plant?
Ornamental grasses are popular with the staff at Ted's because of their diverse character, uses, and forgiving nature.

Central Iowa

CL

TimberPine Nursery & Greenhouse
18863 Jewell Drive
Earlham, IA 50072 *Madison*
515-834-2712
sales@timberpine.com
www.timberpine.com

When are they there? Year-round. Monday-Saturday, Sunday.
What are their hours? 8:00 AM to 5:00 PM, 12:00 PM to 4:00 PM.

Get to know them:
TimberPine Nursery is located on 120 acres in Dallas County, just a short drive from the Des Moines metro. Much of their product line is grown on site including their trees, shrubs, and perennials. Visitors have the opportunity to see production techniques in action while browsing nursery stock for sale. Best of all, the people who grow the plants are there to help answer your questions.

Specialties:
Thousands of trees are TimberPine's specialty, making it possibly the largest selection in central Iowa. Plenty of walking paths lead visitors through areas of trees, shrubs, and perennials planted in garden settings. The company also operates a landscape design and build service.

Central Iowa

CL

Town & Country Market
Larry Larson
308 Main St.
Slater, IA 50244 *Story*
515-228-3131

When are they there? Year-round. Daily.
What are their hours? Call for open hours.

Specialties:
At Town & Country Market you'll find hardy shrub roses for the Midwest including Griffith Buck roses. Unique perennials, especially ones for the shade, and annuals are also in stock.

Central Iowa

CL Other Places of Interest in the Central Iowa Region

Better Homes &
Gardens Test Garden
Sandra Gerdes
1716 Locust Street
Des Moines, IA 50309 *Polk*
sandra.gerdes@meredith.com
www.bhg.com/gardening/design/
test-garden-secrets/visiting-the-
test-garden.

Buxton Park
City of Indianola
Dept. of Parks & Recreation
2204 West 2nd Avenue
Indianola, IA 50125 *Warren*

164

Central Iowa

CL

Country Landscapes
Jim Mason
56985 Lincoln Highway
Ames, IA 50010 *Story*
800-794-9795

Cox's Greenhouse
Roy & Janet Cox
1008 North 11th Avenue East
Newton, IA 50208 *Jasper*
641-792-3015

Des Moines Botanical Center
Dawn Goodrich
909 Robert D. Ray Dr
Des Moines, IA 50316 *Polk*
515-323-6290
www.botanicalcenter.org

Dillon Plant Company
Craig Jacobson
2554 Dillon Rd.
Marshalltown, IA 50158 *Marshall*
641-479-2632

Ewing Park Lilac Arboretum
City of Des Moines
Department of Parks
909 E. River Dr.
Des Moines, IA 50316 *Polk*
515-242-2934

Fusion Daylilies
12 West High Street
Marshalltown, IA 50158 *Marshall*
641-752-2264

Garden Gate Magazine Test Garden
Marcia Leeper
2200 Grand Avenue
Des Moines, IA 50312 *Polk*
800-341-4769

Great Plains Garden Center
4365 NE 44th Drive
Des Moines, IA 50317 *Polk*
515-265-6058

Heard Gardens
Carrie Wolfe
8000 Raccoon River Drive
West Des Moines, IA 50266 *Polk*
515-987-0800
www.heardgardens.com

Herbs-Liscious
1702 South Sixth Street
Marshalltown, IA 50158 *Marshall*
515-752-4976

Central Iowa

CL

Herndon's Des Moines Seed &
Nursery Company
6015 Grand Avenue
Des Moines, IA 50312 *Polk*
515-274-2586

High Hopes Gardens
2860 Knapp Ave.
Melbourne, IA 50162 *Marshall*
641-482-3185

Holub Gardens, Inc.
Jerry Holub
6125 Merle Hay Road
Johnston, IA 50131 *Polk*
515-278-8600
www.holubs.com

Hostahaven.com Gardens
Andrew Lietzow
1250 41st Street
Des Moines, IA 50311 *Polk*
515-274-0300

Iowa Outdoor Products
3200 86th Street
Des Moines, IA 50322 *Polk*
515-277-6242
www.iowaoutdoorproducts.com

Knight & Sons Nursery
3556 L Lane
Adel, IA 50003 *Dallas*
515-834-9092

Lowe-Berry Garden Center & Floral
2204 Mamie Eisenhower Street
Boone, IA 50036 *Boone*
515-432-6275

Miller Nursery Co.
James Poulson & John Mickey
5155 NW 57th Ave.
Johnston, IA 50131 *Polk*
515-276-7505
admin@millernursery.com
www.millernursery.com

Pella Nursery
Steve Vermeer
1809 Vermeer Road East
Pella, IA 50219 *Marion*
641-628-1285

Quilted Gardens
Barry Laws & Larry Skellenger
1626 Evergreen Ave.
Des Moines, IA 50320 *Polk*
515-288-6768
www.quiltedgardens.com

Central Iowa

CL

Red Maple Greenhouse
3511 White Pole Road
Dexter, IA 50070 *Dallas*
515-789-4580

Renes Greenhouse
1444 East Washington Ave.
Des Moines, IA 50316 *Polk*
515-266-0267

Scholte House
728 Washington Street
Pella, IA 50219 *Marion*
641-628-3684

Split Rail Gardens
Elsie Morris
1989 US Hwy. 69, PO Box 43
Osceola, IA 50213 *Clarke*

The Garden Center
17379 G58 Highway
Milo, IA 50166 *Warren*
641-942-6229

Timbercreek Gardens
2586 250th Street
Marshalltown, IA 50158 *Marshall*
641-752-6807

TNT Landscaping & Nursery
Bret Wram
1313 SW Ordnance Road
Ankeny, IA 50021 *Polk*
515-965-1206
wramfamily@msn.com

Vic Scott Landscaping & Nursery
6799 NE 14th Street
Ankeny, IA 50021 *Polk*
515-289-1070

Wildflowers from Nature's Way
Dorothy Baringer
3162 Ray Street
Woodburn, IA 50275 *Clarke*

Woodsmith Store Garden Center
10320 Hickman Road
Clive, IA 50325 *Polk*

Marvin's Victory Gardens
Marvin & Issy Lemke
3615 Davisson Road
Des Moines, IA 50310 *Polk*
515-255-4295
lemkeiowa@aol.com

Central Iowa

Your Day Trip Planner for *Central Iowa*

I can't think of any gardener who wouldn't want to steal away at least one day in spring with a band of co-horts to take in sites of horticultural interest. But where to go can be a most vexing question with so many gardens and so little time. That's why I've composed the following day trip planner to assist you in your preparations for a day afield enjoying the bounty of Iowa's garden attractions. Though you're certainly free to put your own together, I thought you might enjoy this trip that I took once.

Best time of year: Spring
Estimated round-trip mileage: 64 miles
Number of places: 3

Having spent a few years of my life in Ames, I'm awfully fond of it, but particularly so for the little things that can keep a gardener occupied here. Start off with **Reiman Gardens**. It's practically a rite of passage for most Iowa gardeners. I remember growing up and being asked that prying question "Have you been to Reiman Gardens?" Until I was about 14, I sheepishly answered no. For many it's still an untapped resource, especially if you don't make it to Ames often. But Reiman has more to offer than just 14 acres of grounds landscaped in different styles and themes. The conservatory and Christina Reiman Butterfly Wing are popular attractions and draw in thousands of visitors annually. Let a butterfly tickle your hand, enjoy the rainforest-like conditions of the conservatory, and browse bed after bed of perennials. There's something to keep everyone in your group interested.

Central Iowa

CL

I could employ some cliché about ideas and plants but really it's just time to buy things. I love public gardens but I've usually got to satisfy my urge to spend something come day's end. If you're in town on a weekend in May, you'd be wise to mosey out north of Ames to a little development across the road and up the hill from Ada Hayden Heritage Park. Called **Skycrest Gardens**, this tucked-away nursery is scenically nestled amongst tall trees and comely houses, all of which weren't there when the nursery began some 20 years ago. Operated by Tom and Marilyn Kinney, Skycrest is a draw for hosta collectors and water gardeners. Five water gardens and a large show bed of hostas, which have been featured on several regional garden tours, join winding island beds filled with favorite perennials and annuals to create a picturesque piece of heaven on earth. This is easily Ames' best kept gardening secret, but it doesn't have to be. Pay them a visit and see what you'll find (and it sure won't be any weeds!)

I think I could write an entire guide on food in Ames alone. For a small Midwestern city, Ames offers food-seeking visitors a boastful menu. But my favorite is easily The Café [(515) 292-0100], a progressive new concept in restaurants that's catching on across the country. At The Café they specialize in using locally grown produce fruits, vegetables, meats, and cheeses. The menu, while loaded with earthy Midwestern goodness, transcends home-style and gives fine dining an accessible and affordable ambiance. Don't forget the dessert case!

After tickling the taste buds, it's off to another public garden. When you've got so many to enjoy in central Iowa why not, right? Plus it's easy on the pocketbook if you're watching the spending (or someone else in your household is). The **Iowa**

Central Iowa

CL

Arboretum appropriately bills itself as a living library of plants. Located north of Madrid, the arboretum is a fine place to spend the afternoon in a relaxing environment among trees that will happily uptake the generous output of carbon dioxide you'll produce from your post-lunch walk. You've always looked for the perfect excuse for dessert. It helps the trees grow.

Come back to the arboretum later in the fall to enjoy a spectacular fall color display, not only of the trees but of the impressive collection of ornamental grasses assembled by volunteers over the last several years. They even host an ornamental grass sale in mid-September if you're in search of a few good blades to accent your fall garden.

Best time of year: Summer
Estimated round-trip mileage: 124 miles
Number of places: 3

If you're thinking about taking an early lunch and getting a head start on the weekend, why not start in Des Moines at the **Better Homes and Gardens® Test Garden**? Open on Fridays from noon until 2:00 PM, this immaculate show garden is the site of many photo shoots for magazines published by the Meredith Corporation. Managed by Sandra Gerdes and maintained by a staff of no more than three, the Test Garden is the premier place in Iowa to garner ideas directly from the pros and to see the latest and greatest new plants under real world conditions right in our own state. If you don't see something you were looking for, ask Sandra. Chances are it's already been axed!

Just down the street on Grand Avenue is a local fixture. **Herndon's Des Moines Seed and Nursery Company** offers a full-line of nursery stock including many of the newer varieties you maybe just saw at the BHG® Test Garden. But their pottery selection is to die for. Stocking the latest fashions from class-act manufacturers like Campania, you'll find a patio's worth of must-have containers. Container gardeners beware!

But suppose container gardening isn't your thing. If hostas get you going, you'll want to hit the road for **Flying Frog Hosta Farm** located a short drive south of Des Moines in the countryside north of Indianola. Their collection of just over 700 cultivars leaves nothing to be desired, other than an expansive yard for one of each. Even if you're not a collector, Marsha Ansevics and husband Bruno can help you find a few hostas for tucking in and about your shade garden. They might even suggest a pulmonaria or heuchera or two to go with them. And if you're feeling guilty because your friends at work couldn't make it along, you can pick them up a little gift from Marsha's "Garden Shed." If you're in search of a place to host your next Master Gardener or garden club outing, Marsha and Bruno would welcome your inquiry. After all, as they put it, "gardeners are just the best."

With the afternoon drawing nigh, it might seem appropriate to cap the day off (and kick the weekend into high gear), with a little wine tasting at Southern Hills Winery [(641) 342-2808] in Osceola. Located just off Interstate 35, they carry a wide assortment of fruit wines with catchy names like Kick and a Pat (a blend of 'Niagara', 'Diamond', and 'Brianna' grapes) and You're Making Me Blush (a blend of 'Elvira' grapes and red raspberries). Take a bottle home to share with the spouse (or keep for yourself!)

Notes

Travelogue

Notes

Notes

Travelogue

Notes

Travelogue

Notes

Travelogue

Notes

Travelogue

Notes

Notes

Notes

Notes

Travelogue

Notes

Travelogue

Notes

Travelogue

Notes

Travelogue

Notes

Notes

Travelogue

Notes

Notes

Travelogue

Notes

Notes

Notes